Praise for *Let's Choose Less*

Let's Choose Less by Jenna Michael is an invaluable resource for anyone navigating the complexities of parenthood. I first delved into its practical and tactical advice while pregnant and reread it in my early postpartum days. I found its realistic perspective to be a refreshing change compared to other parenting books that left me feeling overwhelmed. The book's wealth of resources and handy lists make it easy to reference, ensuring that I can continually revisit its insights for years to come. It's a must-read for anyone seeking a grounded approach to parenting that emphasizes simplicity and effectiveness.

—**Bridget Kelly Sinha,** doctor of physical therapy, founder of Balanced Physical Therapy, and mother

Jenna is a bold lioness in a culture that screams more. Less? Yes, less, but not less of spirit, love, or grace. Less of the demands of a world we don't live for. Less clutter, less stuff, less business, less demands, and less cultural standards. Physically less stuff!

In her book, she offers you the freedom to choose less for your family—to intentionally pick up in strength the reins and enter the driver's seat for what is internationally less and best for those who call your house home.

Jenna helps you navigate pregnancy, postpartum, the toddler years, and beyond. She skillfully equips you with the tools to go against the grain and consume only what is needed for you specifically. She strips away the "perfect" picture of motherhood and offers you a real-life guidebook full of knowledge written by a real mom.

By choosing less, you will ultimately gain so much more.

—**Nichole Thompson,** mother and author of *The Miscarriage Journal*

Bingo! As you think, plan, and execute on lifestyle choices for your unique family, here's a helpful tool that will allow you to simplify and spend your time on the things you value. Jenna's helpful lists and simple organizational tools do the heavy lifting for you. She encourages your creativity, based on your family values and priorities, and her warm style, stories, and encouragement make it easy to get started building a family structure that works for you!

—**Linda Reeb,** mother, grandmother, author of *Wise Moms*, and founder of Moms Mentoring

Jenna goes above and beyond to guide families toward a life of fullness and meaning—without the clutter. Her insights help readers shift their mindset, focus on their family's core values, and build a home that truly supports their well-being. I want to gift this book to every new family—it's a game-changer!

—**Alexis Bonsall,** mother of three, certified parent coach, and founder of Thriving Parenthood

Jenna has written a deeply authentic and transformative guide to parenting with intention Her words resonate because she truly lives the principles she shares, embodying a life of freedom and joy through minimalism. This book challenges the overwhelming noise of social media and offers a refreshing vision of what parenting can look like when we embrace less. Reading it has inspired me to streamline my own life—paring down material possessions and aligning our family's values and schedule with what truly matters. Jenna's message is not just practical but profoundly freeing, making this a must-read for anyone seeking to parent with purpose.

—**Amanda Lea,** mother, writer, and communications advisor

Let's Choose Less is engaging and easy to read while also exercising my mom brain in a supportive and loving way. I like how the book can be read in approachable bites to learn a new skill or focus on a certain time in parenting. I read this book before the holiday season, and it empowered me to implement an essentialism approach to the season. As a mom of three, I've been overwhelmed and feel like I may need a redo on how to approach parenting. But, with a lot of encouragement from Jenna's book, I'm starting to find new areas to pare down and refocus on our family values.

—**Eva Squibb,** mother, family nurse practitioner

LET'S CHOOSE

LESS

LET'S
CHOOSE
LESS

A YOUNG FAMILY'S

GUIDE TO SIMPLY LIVING

JENNA MICHAEL

For Jonathan

Without you, there would be no us.

Without us, there would be no them.

You are the cornerstone.

TABLE OF CONTENTS

PART ONE

LET'S CHOOSE LESS
BASICS

3

INTRODUCTION

———

Buckle Up.

I t's a Saturday afternoon, the weather is picture-perfect, my husband is playing in the yard with the older kids while our toddler naps, and I am hiding in my closet with my computer. Yes, hiding. My full-time job is to raise four beautiful kids who as of this moment are all under the age of eight and unusually skilled at finding me when they want something. By day I am a stay-at-home mom. I homeschool our oldest kids, love to read, and think exercise and coffee are vital parts of life. In the cracks of motherhood, those stolen moments where we fill our time with something that reminds us of what we were like before we became "Mom," I wrote this book.

I drafted chapters while fielding snack requests. I made lists while sitting in the hallway waiting for someone to finally fall asleep so I could too. Many times, I wrote while not able to see the screen because a small person was in my lap between me and my computer. I quizzed my friends about motherhood during playdates. Nap times, weekend afternoons, early mornings before anyone was awake, the precious moments when Elsa entertained kids for the millionth time, or evenings while my husband handled bedtime, I typed away at my computer. The words on these pages were written while real motherhood was happening. As any parent knows, working while raising kids feels a lot like trying to climb a muddy hill in a thunderstorm. Yet somehow, here we are. What better time to write a lifestyle manual for families with young kids than when you are in the middle of parenting little kids? I'd say there isn't one, so I did.

Welcome to *Let's Choose Less*—where the coffee is usually lukewarm, the laundry needs to be folded, you might accidentally step on a toy train, and the love is tangible. This is not your average parenting book. It's a book for real moms, written by a real mom. It's meant for moms entering motherhood or somewhere in the throes of it. We will cover how to define your values, what you don't need to add on your baby registry, guides for parenting kids from birth through age five, how to pursue less clutter in your home and your calendar, and how to take it all on the go. You can read cover to cover, or you can choose different sections to read on your own. It's meant to be picked up and put down while you kiss a boo-boo, accidentally fall asleep sitting up, or reheat your coffee (again). I hope it gets covered in crumbs, milk stains, and accidental crayon doodles. It was created during real life, and it is meant to be read that way as well.

Let's Choose Less follows the story of how our family accidentally discovered our purpose. It isn't perfect because neither are we. The goal is to take pressure off of parents. To let you know that it's OK if you're tired and stressed out by all the kid clutter. That you don't have to agree with everything you hear when it comes to raising kids, especially if it comes from a well-meaning stranger in the salad dressing aisle of the grocery store or from someone on the internet. A University of California study found that the United States is home to 3.1 percent of the world's children but is responsible for 40 percent of the world's toy consumption,[1] so I'm here to change that.

Dog-ear pages, circle, underline, talk to your friends, and write in the margins. Read when you can and take your time. Better yet, read it out loud with your best friend or your spouse. Live with the book the way I have lived with it while writing. At one point I had to stop writing because I was so burned out in daily parenting that writing about parenting in my limited free time seemed impossible. If it's too much, take a break and come back when you're ready. Motherhood is complicated enough, and your parenting books shouldn't add to the confusion. Dive in and *Let's Choose Less* together.

Buckle up, girlfriend; we are about to become best friends.

---

1 Jeanne E. Arnold, Anthony Graesch, Enzo Ragazzini, and Elinor Ochs, *Life at Home in the Twenty-First Century: 32 Families Open Their Doors* (The Cotsen Institute of Archaeology Press, 2017). See also https://www.uctv.tv/RelatedContent. aspx?RelatedID=301#:~:text=Women%20who%20are%20bothered%20by,with%20 the%20entire%20family%20together.

CHAPTER 1

OUR STORY

You must get rid of the excess to be able to have more.

One of the most embarrassing things I've ever done as a parent happened approximately forty-eight hours into my parenting journey. My husband, Jonathan, and I were about to be discharged from the hospital with our first baby, and the nurse was finishing her hourlong lecture on how to care for our newborn daughter. Our eyes were glassy, we hadn't slept, and we were absorbing nothing she said. Bless her heart, our nurse was trying to be helpful and teach us how to take care of this new person we were responsible for, but we heard absolutely nothing, and all we wanted was to go home.

After finally getting permission to leave, I had one last question: "Do we need to sign a deed or anything before we leave?" The nurse just looked at us and rather unkindly said, "No, this is *your* baby. Now you go home and raise her."

As much as I cringe every time I tell the story, it's the perfect example of how unprepared I was for motherhood. Also, in case you're wondering, the answer is no—there is no deed to your child.

Babies are born innately themselves. From day one, you can tell their little personalities, and they just become more themselves over time. Emily was born completely bald but full of personality. Today she has amazing curly hair, and her personality is just as large and in charge as it was when she was born.

In the hospital room after she was delivered, I couldn't take my eyes off her. Somehow this little person was ours, and I was completely overwhelmed with equal parts terror and love. Emily has never needed much sleep, and this was apparent from the beginning. While we were figuring out how to make our exit from the hospital, I was more tired than I ever knew possible, and that's where my mistake about a baby deed came in. Either way, we made it home, and I launched myself full force into motherhood. I was prepared, wasn't I?

When I was a kid and someone would ask me what I wanted to be when I grew up, my response was always, "I want to be [whatever sounded interesting to me at the time]." But I would always follow it up with: 'But then I'll have lots of babies."

I'm the oldest of five girls. Yes, five girls. (And before you say it, don't feel bad for my dad.) Our house was loud and full of all the chaos you can imagine with that many kids who all shared a love for dance. We had an entire closet full of dance costumes, and we did laundry in lights, darks, and pinks. The food was always spectacular, and we were all usually talking at the same time. It was wonderful, and I loved it so much that I wanted the same thing in my own version.

After high school, I went to college at Elon University to major in dance. One summer I decided to get ahead in some general education class requirements, so I stayed on campus for summer school and to work at my new job in the admissions office as a tour guide. On the first day of my new job, I walked into a room of people I didn't know and met the love of my life. (Cue the Hallmark music.) Jonathan—aka Jon the dream boat with the black backpack and orange juice in a coffee mug—was in charge of training the new tour guides that day. So I played dumb for everything. At each part of learning the job, I asked for extra help, and somehow my plan worked like a charm. Almost immediately we were spending all our free time together, and within two weeks we were dating.

As rising junior and seniors in college, we were remarkably young to know where we wanted our lives to go, but that didn't stop us from making plans. Two years after we met (almost to the day), we were engaged. We got married fifteen months after that. Young enough that folks raised their eyebrows at us for getting married at twenty-three and twenty-four, but our answer was always the same: we just knew.

Not long after anyone gets married, it's common for all the questions about having kids to start rolling in. My answer was always that having babies was my calling, and I wanted them pronto. Jobs and adventures took us to a few different locations before finally in 2016 it was time to start our family. To say I was ready would be an understatement. This was something I had been dreaming of my whole life, and now suddenly it was happening.

From the moment the two lines showed up on the pregnancy test, I was in full "motherhood preparation mode." We moved across the country to live close to our family, and I started devouring parenting books, magazines, websites, Pinterest boards, blogs, and anything else I could get my hands on that would make me the best mom ever.

Jon read exactly one book. I couldn't get over how he wasn't doing more to prepare; his response was always, "We will figure it out!" Um, NO. This was major and we needed to PREPARE. We took multiple childbirth classes, toured the hospital, interviewed pediatricians, and packed a hospital bag the size of Kansas exactly halfway through my pregnancy. It was as if I were preparing for the world's largest event EVER, but it was only happening to us. (I didn't expect everyone else to pack a Kansas-sized hospital bag for the delivery of our first child, obviously.) At our final dinner before we welcomed our baby into the world, I famously said, "This is the last dinner out we will ever get to have." Jon, of course, rolled his eyes and told me to eat my burger. I may have been a little dramatic in my preparations, but you get my drift. We were having a baby, and we needed to be ready. And then Emily was born.

Motherhood is supposed to be completely natural—that's what everyone says, right? It's what I had always dreamed of, yet I felt like I wasn't doing it right. But how was that possible? I read all the books, I followed all the guides, I registered for all the gadgets, yet I still felt like a fish out of water. We were renting a two-bedroom townhouse at the time, and it was just the right amount of space when we moved in. Our perfectly sized home very quickly filled to the brim with things—mostly baby related. I'm embarrassed to admit that we needed to store what we couldn't fit at our place at my parent's house and at my in-laws. Yes, both locations.

Our possessions seemed to constantly multiply despite our best efforts not to accumulate more. Clothes that were too small, bottle parts, breastfeeding supplies, random gifts people would graciously drop off, spare baby gear, strollers (don't even get me started on strollers), car seats, and toys—all for one tiny baby! Not to mention pregnancy clothes for each season, breastfeeding clothes for each season, multiple sizes of clothes as I went through my postpartum journey, and all the other junk we owned as well. We were drowning in things, and my full-time job was to manage all of it on top of taking care of a small human.

There had to be an easier way. Was it like this for everyone?
Exactly nine months after delivering Emily, I found out we were having another baby. It was time to find an answer.

After months of house hunting, we bought our first home. Four bedrooms, two living rooms, a newly renovated kitchen, a basement for playing, a huge backyard, a garage, and a storage area perfect for a spare fridge. We moved in with a townhouse amount of stuff and had more than enough room to spare.

"This is all the space we will ever need." Famous words of a pregnant woman who has no idea what she's talking about. Two weeks after moving in, our sweet Sophie was born. Now, with two kids under the age of two and a whole house to unpack, I was up to the challenge, wasn't I? Debatable. It took months to come out from under the newborn fog and the unpacked boxes to even begin trying to figure out where to store things. We had all this new storage space, and I was flabbergasted at how quickly our new house filled up. Two kids meant twice as much stuff, yet I was no more prepared for dealing with the stuff this time around than the first time. No corner was safe from a storage bin, and every single closet was stacked floor to ceiling with stuff. Baby clothes and toys were piled up in hallways, and anything that could fit under beds was shoved in and quickly forgotten about.

I was more overwhelmed than ever before, constantly stressed, and I never slowed down. There was always so much to do, and I never seemed to be able to get ahead no matter how hard I worked or how much I prepped in advance. Time to be present and enjoy watching our two little girls grow up together wasn't an option because the laundry needed to be folded and the toys needed to be put away . . . again. By worrying about managing our household, I was missing out on some of the best parts of being a mom. I knew it, but I didn't know how to stop.

On a random evening when Jon and I were out to dinner with a friend, they recommended the book *Essentialism* by Greg McKeown.[2] Jon read it first and then suggested I read it next. When I finally got around to doing so, because I was so busy keeping up with our house and our kids, I couldn't put it down. Suddenly, the proverbial light bulb over our heads clicked on.

Essentialism repeatedly mentions the idea that if you don't choose to prioritize your life, something else will. In our circumstance, clutter was prioritizing our lives. Essentialism in its simplest form means having only what you need and not living in excess in all aspects of your life. It means managing the extra and controlling what comes in and out of your house—with an emphasis on quality over quantity. It is a lifestyle that actively pursues "less" in all aspects of living. Essentialism encompasses physical clutter like the side of your garage you avoid looking at each time you open the

2 Greg McKeown, *Essentialism: The Disciplined Pursuit of Less* (New York: Crown Business, 2014).

door. But it also includes mental clutter like having too many commitments on your schedule. Closely related to essentialism is *minimalism*. *Minimalism* was made popular by authors Joshua Fields Millburn and Ryan Nicodemus when they wrote the book *Minimalism: Live a Meaningful Life*[3] about becoming minimalists themselves. Minimalism, per Millburn and Nicodemus, is the practice of owning fewer possessions. Sound familiar? That's because depending on whom you talk to, essentialism and minimalism aren't that different from each other. The concepts are easily morphed in the eye of the beholder. There are small nuances, title changes, varied definitions, and followers who will swear that one is better than the other. Still, at the end of the day, both concepts prioritize clearing room mentally and physically for more.

We were hooked.

The answer I had been looking for was so simple. We were allowing our things, our calendars, and the external societal pressure of what we were supposed to be as parents to dictate how we lived. Our house wasn't too small, and we had plenty of closet space. We just needed to even out the ratio of things we owned to the storage we had. We needed less laundry in our house so there was less to wash all the time. Toys needed to be pared down to a manageable amount so there was less to maintain and clean. Along with a house full of things, we had calendars full of unnecessary commitments

---

3 Joshua Fields Millburn and Ryan Nicodemus, *Minimalism: Live a Meaningful Life* (Asymmetrical Press, 2011).

that left us with no extra time for our family or relaxation. It was like getting glasses for the first time and seeing the world from a completely new perspective. It was a game changer, yet we had no idea how to implement this incredible concept. In theory, it all sounded spectacular. But how were we going to get there?

We started in the easiest place possible: the playroom. We researched what kinds of toys we wanted for our family, and if something didn't fall into those parameters, it was automatically added to the donation pile. From there, we did one drawer or one closet at a time. I stopped buying baby clothes in bulk and started looking into capsule wardrobes for our kids. (We'll talk more about capsule wardrobes soon!) We began the practice of asking ourselves if an item was necessary before we allowed it into our home. Anything that was allowed to enter needed an immediate "place to live." If there wasn't an obvious location, we either didn't need it or we had to "say goodbye" to something else.

Purchases became about quality over quantity, and instead of buying several of something, we would invest in one or two really good versions. Yoga pants were a big one for me. As someone who exercises regularly, it was stressful to tackle my athletic wear drawer. I removed all the mediocre options and replaced them with only high-quality options. Instead of having to frequently replace my midbrand yoga pants when they inevitably wore out or stretched out, I invested in several higher quality options. I haven't had to buy new yoga pants since before the pandemic. Quality over quantity.

In time, editing our belongings felt like a muscle we were strengthening. It became easier to decide if something was important or if it needed to go, and it became increasingly easier to let go of things. Once we finished an area or a project list, we would go back and start again. There was always more that could go because there was always more we were learning.

Donations were heaved out the door in massive quantities—and my parents and sisters thought I was crazy.

I come from a family of savers from all sides—the kind of people who keep things "just in case." It makes sense. My grandparents were Depression Era babies, so everything was saved because there may not have been the ability to get more later. My grandma used to collect fancy soaps in the shape of shells that were only ever to be used when guests came over. As she aged, things like tissue boxes, scissors, pens, and checkbooks were nonnegotiables that had to be saved in large quantities. In her mind, you never knew when you might need those items or if it would be hard to get more of them. After she passed, we found cookies hidden in all kinds of places around her house. She never wanted to run out. (I can't blame her. Who would want to be without cookies?) This mindset carried over to their kids—aka my parents—and into my childhood. (Although to my knowledge, no one else I'm related to has hidden cookies in their home yet.)

As a kid, I saved everything because that was what my whole family did. I was a musical theater kid, and I saved every script, musical score, notebook full of stage directions or feedback, CD soundtrack, and T-shirt from every show I was ever in. Old notes I passed back and forth with a friend in middle school, my favorite shirts from elementary school, every trophy I ever received, every test I ever took, my high school anatomy textbook, and the list goes on. (Seriously, why did I think I would need to reference textbooks?) Piles of things were stored in bins or boxes just waiting for the day I *might* need them or want to look at them again. But not unsurprisingly, I never did. So they just took up space and gathered dust.

After I got married, my mom was ready to let me be in charge of all my childhood treasures. So Jon and I ventured up to the attic in my parents' house to see how much we would be storing in our little townhouse. There were SEVEN oversized plastic bins of things I had deemed "important" over my childhood and put aside to save. There were also boxes my mom had kindly saved for me along with all the junk that was still lurking in the back of my childhood closet. It was embarrassing to watch my dad and my new husband struggle to lift these massive containers full of junk, yet I still saved them for years. Once we removed all the bins from my parents' house, they took up valuable storage space in our first home. I'm sure this is one of many reasons we ran out of room so quickly.

Years after we started living a more minimal lifestyle, I finally sifted through all my childhood bins. It took months, and it was truly an overwhelming process, so I could only do a small bit at a time. As I sifted through all I'd saved, very little ended up in the "essentials" pile. My kindergarten backpack ended up in the kids' dress-up bin, paper clutter was recycled, and anything broken or unrecognizable was removed. In the end, I consolidated everything down to one bin that now lives in our attic—and it's still likely way too much. (Mental note to add it to my project list to go back through this again soon.) Of all the things I've "said goodbye" to on this journey, I can't remember a single item I've regretted getting rid of. And I'm for sure not missing my middle school math tests.

Maggie, our third little girl, was born in 2020, and things were far less complicated inside our home than in our past "new baby" experiences. Even though it was 2020 (ahem, COVID-19), having another baby during the height of a pandemic was less overwhelming because we knew how much we actually needed for a newborn this time around. We were living differently, and the results were right in front of us. Our diaper bag was smaller than it had ever been, even though we now needed a minivan to cart all our little people around. Maggie had far fewer clothes than our other kids, but all this did was make things easier. We were onto something, and it was working.

Along with editing our physical belongings, we expanded our process from closets and drawers to our calendars, our finances, our household values, and our social commitments. Our family identified what was most important to us—at the time, it was princesses for Emily and Sophie—and together we built a family value statement surrounding those beliefs. (You'll get to learn more about this later in the book.)

Our framework was that if someone looked at our calendar or our finances, they would be able to tell what was most important to us. We began to build off what we learned from *Essentialism* and clearing out clutter to form a new lifestyle and mindset for our family. Finally we were in control of our home, our belongings, and our lives. *Let's Choose Less* was born.

Clutter is directly related to stress, anxiety, and decreased productivity. The things we bring into our homes *literally* affect our health. They signal to our brain that we can't relax, which causes our sensory systems to overload, and we are never truly able to calm down.

Neuroscience News states that "a cluttered environment can lead to cognitive overload, as the brain struggles to prioritize attention amidst distractions."[4] And women are far more affected by clutter-induced stress than men. No wonder I was so overwhelmed as a new mom trying to find my way! I was surrounded by clutter on all sides.

---

4 Erika Penney, "Why Household Mess Triggers Stress and Anxiety," September 4, 2023, Neuroscience News, https://neurosciencenews.com/anxiety-stress-messy-home-23874.

The average American home contains around 300,000 items,[5] yet at least 25 percent of Americans with two-car garages don't have room to park a car inside, and only one-third can park one car in their garages due to clutter.[6] Turns out I wasn't alone in my struggles with clutter.

Clutter attracts clutter, so the more we have, the greater the problem grows. Too much stuff makes us anxious and can inhibit our decision-making processes. We aren't sure we will ever get that mountain of laundry finished, so why not just leave it for another time? It can make us feel guilty or even ashamed of the state of our home and hesitant to invite anyone over. It causes frustration when we can't find our keys in the pile of mail on the home office desk or two matching socks for our kid while we are already running late for the day. No one has ever said, "I love a mess; it's so relaxing!"

Our homes are where we are supposed to be relaxed, but they are adding to our stress load.

We already know that as parents our time to relax is limited, and limited doesn't even really encompass how rare it is to have a quiet evening when no one wakes up or gets out of

5 Mary MacVean, "For Many People, Gathering Possessions Is Just the Stuff of Life," March 21, 2014, *Los Angeles Times*, https://www.latimes.com/health/la-xpm-2014-mar-21-la-he-keeping-stuff-20140322-story.html.

6 Garage Goals Quiz, https://www.garageliving.com/blog/2023-garage-goals-quiz?utm_campaign=Q4%202022%20-%20Garage%20Goals&utm_term=Facebook&utm_content=230307076&utm_medium=social&utm_source=facebook&hss_channel=fbp-798048963704620.

bed. If our downtime is already this precious, why are we con-
taminating it with external stimuli that are *within* our control?
(Because we know our kids are not within our control when
it comes to free time—EVER.)

Let's Choose Less takes the edge off the excess. By eliminating the mountain of toys, cleaning up is a little easier.
Reducing the amount of clothes in everyone's closet cuts down
on the amount of clothes strewn about the house and needing
to be washed. Less calendar commitments and household
chores reduce our mental load, and we just might be able to
relax a little more. We think hard before buying something
because it will need a place to go in our home or we will
have to get rid of something else to make room for the new
item. This doesn't mean we don't own anything—just what
is needed.

Let's Choose Less is entirely personal and can vary
depending on the individual. Our family is full of avid readers,
so we have books everywhere. What is just the right number of
books for me might be nowhere near enough for you. Maybe
your family is really into LEGOs, so what would be a very
stressful amount of LEGO bricks for me might be just right
for you. I have an affinity for books, bags, and athletic wear
that borders on unhealthy. You do you.

Jay, our fourth and final kiddo, was born in 2021, and we
finally did run out of room in our first house. There was no
way we were going to be able to convince Emily, Sophie, and
Maggie to share a bedroom with one closet for the rest of their
lives. Enter house number two—our long-term, forever home.

We were able to move confidently knowing our family had the tools to maintain our principles while adjusting to a new home. We weren't looking for more space for our things, but physical space for our kids to sleep. We moved into our new home intending to leave drawers empty in the kitchen, remove shelves in closets for more open space, and the mindset that empty space does not have to be filled. To this day, we have been successful with our intentions.

If there's a mess in front of me, you can bet that I won't be able to stare at it and not care. My house is never perfectly clean, but it is always *easy* to clean. Once we started living with the *Let's Choose Less* principles, I was finally able to slow down and enjoy more of the little moments in motherhood. Our house can be tidied in ten minutes. We make it fun to see how fast we can go or blast music throughout the house to dance while we clean. If it's just me tidying, it's still easy. Everything has a place, so it's just a matter of getting items to where they go. This doesn't mean we don't have stuff or that our house doesn't get messy; it just means that it's a little easier to manage the inevitable mess. My workload as a mom of four kids is significantly reduced from the version of me before we pared down. Not only did we simplify physically, but I also simplified my mental load, which has made me a happier and more present mom.

Y'all, I have four kids. If I can do this, anyone can. If you create the framework, all you have do is live within your self-imposed boundaries. I'm here to help you start. Maybe it's a drawer or your diaper bag, and then you move to the big stuff when you're ready—such as your values, schedule, or closet. The end goal isn't perfection but progress.

As Myquillen Smith says in her book *Cozy Minimalist Home*,[7] our things can turn us into full-time "stuff managers." Putting things away, moving them around, washing clothes, and taking care of the clutter inside our homes takes time away from more important things like enjoying time with our family, taking care of ourselves, making delicious food, or spending quality time relaxing. When we invest all our time and energy into managing our stuff, it takes away from all the other things we can be doing that are probably way more fun. Instead of doing laundry, we could be outside playing. Instead of having to take a lot of time cleaning up all our toys, we could have more time to play. We can spend more time with our kids or doing things we enjoy and less time managing all the stuff.

This lifestyle is not the easy answer. It is not the path that societal pressure or social media have conditioned us to believe is "correct." We are constantly inundated by ads, our phones, videos, commercials, billboards, our friends, and millions of other stimuli to believe that more is better. *Let's Choose Less*

---

7 Myquillen Smith, *Cozy Minimalist Home: More Style, Less Stuff* (Grand Rapids, MI: Zondervan, 2018).

requires going against the grain in today's world and saying "no" to what seems normal to most. In adapting this mindset, you take a brave stance against what every brand, ad agency, influencer, store, and business wants you to do—which is to buy more things.

As a society, we have been conditioned to prioritize our things and let them control our lives. It's time to change that narrative. In gardening, you must prune back the growth to allow for more growth in the future.

You must get rid of the excess to be able to have more.

Let's Choose Less is the same. When you say "no" to excess belongings or commitments, you are choosing to say "yes" to what is most important to you. Instead of saying "yes" to accumulating more stuff, start saying "yes" to decluttering and pursuing a simpler lifestyle so you can focus on having more fun with your family. This is parenthood, guys; the mental load never stops, but if we can lower our workload even marginally, imagine what we could do with all that extra brain power.

I started this journey because I wanted time to focus on remembering the feeling of holding my squishy newborn babies, a sweet little hand that grabs mine when walking down the stairs, or their eyes when they finally realize they know how to read. I wanted to prioritize tickle fights, afternoon coloring sessions, playing in the rain, kissing boo-boos, and making a huge mess in the kitchen together over doing chores or managing household logistics. I refuse to let clutter and things take precious time away from enjoying motherhood. *Let's Choose Less* has opened the doors of possibility for our family while closing the trapdoors of clutter, overwhelm, stress, and overcommitment. We are not perfect. We fall out of habit and need to reevaluate often. But having this framework makes it easy to recalibrate. No more overflowing closets, no more unmanageable mountains of toys, and no more clutter-induced mental health issues. Only freedom to prioritize experiences with our kids and the occasional quiet evening to read a book uninterrupted. *Let's Choose Less* helped my family identify our core values and reduce clutter. I hope it can do the same for yours.

LET'S CHOOSE LESS PRINCIPLES

- ▶ Eliminate excess.
- ▶ Value quality over quantity.
- ▶ Make every purchase with a purpose.
- ▶ Identify your values and stick to them.

Journal Prompt/Discussion Questions:

At the end of each chapter, you'll find a journal prompt section just like this one. My goal is for your family to use these prompts as springboards to inspire deep, meaningful conversations and to home in on what is most important to you as a family. Once you have completed all the prompts, you will have a clear understanding of what your family values are, where your interests lie, and what you can let go of. Feel free to answer separately and then discuss afterward—or go right to the family discussion if that works better for you.

- ► How do you feel about the current state of your home?

- ► Is there a particular part of your home that causes you stress?

- ► What is your least favorite chore?

- ► What is your favorite chore?

- ► Where is the first place you would choose to begin being less?

- ► How much time are you currently spending managing the stuff in your home each week?

CHAPTER 2

DEFINE YOUR FAMILY'S VALUES

Find your GPS.

By fall 2021, our decluttering was in full swing. Our family was settling into our new home, we welcomed our son Jay into the world, and we were prepping for Emily to go to kindergarten the next year. Our lives were very typical for the ages of the kids we had. Emily was in TK (transitional kindergarten) five days a week; Sophie was in the three-year-old class three days a week; Maggie and Jay were at home with me. We were on the go a fair amount between preschool, dance classes, my own work schedule, swim lessons, and soccer games. I was trying my best to keep track of packing lunches, dance shoes, soccer cleats, swim goggles, birthday parties, class parties, and what to make for dinner. They weren't even in elementary school yet, and I already felt overwhelmed with how much was on our calendars. Our home was beautifully decluttered, but our calendar was the complete opposite.

Jon and I stumbled across Emily Oster's book *The Family Firm*[8] where she proposes the concept of running your family the same way you run a business: with a mission statement and a preestablished decision-making process. This sparked a new wave of inspiration for us to use our well-honed decluttering skills in a different way.

The Family Mission Statement

A family mission statement is a clearly defined phrase that focuses on the purpose and principles of a family. Imagine if each household had a distinct purpose with a mission statement leading the way: A clear set of guidelines to establish the boundaries of each family that could easily identify if an answer is yes or no. The ability to immediately identify if something belongs on the boat or should be left behind in the marina. Commitments would be clearly defined, calendar chaos could be easily managed, and families would still have the time to sit down for dinner regularly—should they wish to do so.

All of this from one little phrase? Turns out it's way harder to declutter your schedule than your closet.

In fall 2022, things got even busier despite our best efforts and using our new family mission statement: *Active*

8 Emily Oster, *The Family Firm: A Data-Driven Guide to Better Decision Making in the Early School Years* (New York: Penguin Press, 2021).

bodies, curious minds, grateful hearts. It was a wonderful guide that truly encompassed what we wanted the mission of our family to be, but we had no idea how to implement it into our lives. Between dance classes, soccer practices, swim lessons, school schedules, work responsibilities, family logistics, and household management, Jon and I realized our conversations were always about logistics. We almost never had time to rest let alone spend quality time together. We were floating along knowing we wanted to have a home full of people who loved to be active, learn, and approach all things with an attitude of gratitude. But the final linchpin was missing. We were living with less stuff but leaving little time for things that truly mattered to us like church, travel, or each other.

Jon started attending a weekly men's Bible study group and as part of the group, we went to an event to hear a couple speak in early 2023. Lloyd and Linda Reeb have dedicated their lives to helping others, and Linda, the author of *Wise Moms,*[9] specialized in moms. I was captivated the entire evening, and at the end of the event, I was uncharacteristically brave and approached Linda. She agreed to let me interview her for an article, and thus began a beautiful friendship.

Linda's teachings were like cool water on a hot day. They were refreshing, liberating, and unlike anything I had been able to find in all my reading. She encourages families to live simply and on purpose, to prioritize a marriage-centered family

---

9 Linda Ruth Reeb, *Wise Moms: A Guide for Building Your Home on Christ* (Nashville: HIM Publications, 2024).

instead of a child-focused one, and to dive into important conversations with their spouses on faith and family values. I took my time with our article to glean as much information as I could from our conversations, always wanting to go back and learn more.

I'll never forget sitting in my favorite spot in our house, my reading nook, nestled with notes, and on a FaceTime call with Linda as we finalized the last few details of our article when she asked me a simple question that ultimately became the final cornerstone for *Let's Choose Less*.

"If I looked at your bank account and your calendar, would I be able to tell what is most important to your family?"

Linda and her teachings were the final, missing puzzle pieces to put *Let's Choose Less* in place. She helped us finally succeed in what we were trying to accomplish within our family—and she did it all by asking us one simple question. Every time I hear this question, my heart feels like it surges a little. How could one question so directly hit the nail on the head? Linda wasn't asking what our mission statement or family boundary parameters were (although these are important); she wanted to know if we knew what was most important to our family and whether we were doing anything about it.

Know Your Family Values

Imagine your family is a rowing team. Your boat is your home, and the items on board are the thoughtfully curated items within your home. Your family value system is your GPS. One inaccurate reading could lead your whole operation astray, but with the right heading, the right team, and the right gear, it should be smooth sailing.

Family values are your defining principles or standards that provide moral and ethical direction for your family. Family values take your mission statement and elevate it. Identifying your values creates the framework through which you make all decisions as a family. If something doesn't fall within the parameters of your value system, it's an automatic no. Once you know what your values are, you are more easily able to determine the direction of your family's life, the lifestyle you want to live, the people you prioritize spending time with, how you spend your money, and what you commit to. Your mission statement is a part of your family values, but your values are who you are as a family at your core.

Understanding the importance of your values is the first step; defining and implementing them comes next. Every family is different, so our values may look very different from yours. Values can encompass all kinds of things but the more specific, the better. I doubt that most people would leave kindness or compassion off their list, which are wonderful things to value, but we are going deeper in this process.

Examine each aspect of your life. Are you an inside or an outdoorsy person? Are you a family that loves to eat out, or is home cooking more important? Would you rather do a puzzle or play a board game? Each small detail you can identify will add to your family's understanding of what is most important. Are you a family that loves spending time together, but you find yourself spending all your free time getting to different extracurricular activities? Are weekends for family, but you spend most of them at other kids' birthday parties? Maybe you highly value family time, but your calendar says otherwise. Or maybe your family loves to spend time traveling, but you never have the time because there's always another commitment that takes precedence? As you look beyond the typical values, you'll find the most certain ones stick out more than the others.

Jon and I made it a game. Over a week or so, we each compiled a list of things that were important to us or our family, and at the end of the week, we came together to see where our lists overlapped. It was thrilling to see some major themes emerge, and we immediately recognized that our faith and reading were monumental values in our home. Spending time being active outside, especially together, was also a major contributor. As we whittled away at what we felt our family should look, behave, or be like, we were able to delve into our true, genuine selves.

The more we said no, the clearer our yeses became. Within a few weeks of meeting Linda, we were making huge changes in our lives. We finished all the obligations we had made, but we stopped making new ones. Jon and I started having weekly family strategy meetings to make sure we were aligned on family logistics, home projects, and how each other was doing. Our kids finished the season of whatever activity they were participating in, and then we stopped all extra activities for a full six months. Our calendars had never been emptier. We finished out the school year and then began homeschooling.

I left my current job to pursue a new one. Friendships shifted. We switched churches. Our lives completely changed—and we did too—all because we knew what was most important to us; our faith, our family, reading, and being active outside together. Each of these major changes was terrifying on its own, and yet we were making all of them in quick succession because our paths had never been easier to see.

Suddenly the pressures of society to have kids who excel in all things were gone. We didn't need to sign up for every activity, say yes to every birthday party, or even pursue relationships that didn't add value to our family's lives. It felt invigorating and awful at the same time. Saying no is the hardest yet simplest word. Walking away from a commitment or job that you feel obligated to pursue because "that's what you're supposed to do" is gut-wrenching. Moving out of friendships that don't align with your core values is HARD. But what you gain from leaving the extra weight behind is a new freedom worth far more.

Jon and I went from struggling to find time for each other to carving out weekly strategy meetings for household logistics and taking biannual weekends away for quality time together. Our kids now spend more time together and with us than they ever have before. They are in activities that suit our whole family's schedules and needs, not just their own. Sundays are completely reserved as a Sabbath for only church, family, and rest time. Our family is *thriving*, all because we are doing less of what is expected of us and more of what is important to us.

Make It Fun

Defining your family values can be a fun process to do together, or you can complete different tasks individually and compare your answers later. Each family can and should have a different approach. Maybe you all take the Myers-Briggs (MBTI®) or CliftonStrengths tests, or another personality test of your choice. There are also family values tests you can look up online where you circle different words you find most important. Print one off for each family member and then compare notes to see what you have in common. Jon and I usually take the route of reading every book we can find on the topic and then comparing notes. Or you might find someone like Linda Reed who coaches young mothers! There are plenty of ways to go about finding your values, but no matter how you get there, remember that your family will evolve, so your values may as well.

Pull out your calendar and look at your schedule for this week. Is there anything even remotely related to what you would say is one of your most important values? For a long time, ours were nowhere to be found, but now our values are written all over our schedules. As soon as you identify something inside your value system, let go of anything that doesn't align with it. Every little thing you say no to will be saying yes to something that you truly value. The stronger your commitment to your values, the easier to let go of something that isn't of importance. If you're a family of readers, maybe you don't need to be paying for cable. Are you spending money on something that could be better used elsewhere? If you are a family of foodies, maybe a weekly night out should be scheduled on the calendar.

Once you have clearly defined your values, find a way to prominently display them somewhere in your home where everyone can be reminded of them. There's no limit to how many values should be on the list, but remember we are trying to live with less, so the more concise, the better. This is also where your mission statement can come in handy. Take those values and turn them into a mission statement! Jon and I did it backward. We formed our mission without truly identifying what we valued. Once we listed our values, our mission statement was far more impactful. Get your mission statement printed and turn it into meaningful décor in your home. Refer to your values list and your mission statement as often as you need to.

Your values help establish your family boundaries. When you identify what matters most to your family, it's easy to know what to say no to. Whether that's a calendar commitment, Christmas away from home, a birthday party on a Sunday morning, or too many pairs of socks, your values are the map that guides you through the decision-making process. Boundaries are healthy and can be communicated kindly. As you become more aware of what you need to let go of and where your focus should be when it comes to your money, your calendar, and your commitments, it helps to have a few key phrases ready to make declining an invitation easier. A simple "no" may suffice, but other times you might need to have your wording ready to help ease the cringe that will inevitably happen as you turn down an offer. Here are a few examples:

- ▶ "Thank you so much, but I'm not able to attend."
- ▶ "Our calendar is pretty full right now—hopefully another time."
- ▶ "We have already made our charitable contributions for the year elsewhere. But thank you for the information."
- ▶ "Sundays are for our family, but if there's another day that works for you, we'd love to make that happen!"

Delivery is everything. A "smiling no" with plenty of gratitude can ease the difficulty of saying no. If you know it's the right thing, but it's not an easy no to give, refer to your values list and mission statement to remind yourself of *why* you are declining. Operating from the framework you define will allow you to make decisions habitually. If it isn't within your value system, it's a no, even if it's difficult to turn down. Over time, you'll find that just like your decluttering muscles get stronger, so will your "saying no skills." Take small, incremental steps and keep practicing. You shouldn't turn your entire life around in one day.

How does a well-curated list of family values relate to living a life of less? Your home can and should reflect your values. Maybe your family is like ours, and you don't need a formal dining room. How could you transform the space to be representative of what is most important to you? Your play space is the perfect location to show what kinds of items are valuable. For us, we have children's Bibles all over our home that our kids can and do play with because the Bible is important to us. The items you keep in your home should be there to help you pursue what you value, not keep you from them.

Do you remember the old Tootsie Pop commercial with the kid and the owl? "Mr. Owl, how many licks does it take to get to the center of a Tootsie Pop?" The owl says, "Let's see," and licks three times before biting the whole thing off the stick. This is how it feels to live your life within your family value system while pursuing a life of less physical clutter. You take away all the surface layers to get to the core of what you really want: the center part! You can be free of what society tells you is expected and define your family's parameters for yourself. No one says you must put your kid in four different activities at four years old, but we are made to feel like we are supposed to. There are no laws that say you must say yes to every birthday party invitation, dinner out with friends, or social outing. As Linda Reeb says, "This is your one and only life—how you choose to live it is up to you."

LET'S CHOOSE LESS TIPS FOR IDENTIFYING AND IMPLEMENTING YOUR FAMILY VALUES AND MISSION STATEMENT:

- ▶ Find an online values quiz or personality test that each family member can take individually.
- ▶ Compare answers and see which words continually surface in your conversations.
- ▶ Compile a list of a l your shared values and identify your top values.
- ▶ Use these values to create a family mission statement that can be displayed in your home.
- ▶ Utilize your mission statement and values to decide how to allocate your time, money, and commitments.
- ▶ Create a formula to simplify creating your mission statement.

    a. "We value _____ and commit to _____ as a family."

EXAMPLES OF FAMILY MISSION STATEMENTS:

If you're interested in creating a family mission statement, here are five examples to inspire you:

- ▶ We prioritize kindness, honesty, and respect in all our interactions with one another and the world around us.
- ▶ We value education and personal growth, and we are committed to supporting one another's intellectual and emotional development.
- ▶ We strive to live sustainably and reduce our impact on the environment, and we encourage one another to make choices that align with this goal.
- ▶ We believe in the power of community and are committed to serving those in need, both locally and globally.
- ▶ We prioritize fun, laughter, and quality time together, and we are committed to creating a home filled with love, joy, and connection.

Journal Prompts/Discussion Questions:

▶ What do we enjoy doing together as a family?

▶ What is on our calendar currently that we could say no to?

▶ What is important to us as a family?

▶ Are we spending money on something that doesn't add value to our life?

▶ If I looked at your bank account and your calendar, would I be able to tell what is most important to your family?

▶ If you had more free time in your schedule, what would you spend your time doing?

CHAPTER 3

LET'S CHOOSE LESS IN PRACTICE

Less means more.

L*et's Choose Less* is about choosing to lose. You need to eliminate excess clutter and unnecessary commitments to start winning. Winning here means gaining more time and freedom from obligations, allowing you to focus more on what you want to do rather than what you have to do.

You must start losing to start winning.

People will question your motives and that's OK. Sooner or later they will see that you're onto something, and they might just join you. This is a mindset shift from what you've likely spent your whole life doing, and it will feel uncomfortable. You are creating a new lifestyle, and this won't happen overnight. When Jon and I started clearing things out, our family and friends thought we were ridiculous. It took us years to identify our process and even longer to get into a place where it was habitual, all while feeling like total weirdos in the eyes of everyone we knew.

Even now—years later and with me writing a book about this—we still get questions or comments from those that don't understand us . . . yet! We've questioned ourselves a lot because this was not the way we were raised. *Let's Choose Less* goes against the grain. It asks you to be brave, but trust me, that is a good thing. *Let's Choose Less* is about changing the culture around physical possessions and commitments one family at a time. By refocusing our attention away from consumerism and clutter, we prioritize experiences, time with family or friends, learning, and being present. We are breaking down the boundaries we've been told our whole lives are immovable. And guess what? We can do this.

Less Means More

Let's Choose Less with kids of any age is a little like trying to vacuum while the kids are still eating. Crumbs are falling, but we're just trying to prevent a bigger mess from happening later. This won't result in a perfect home. This won't guarantee your house will never be messy. This is not the easy, fix-all answer to life's greatest mysteries. It is, however, a guide to help make things logistically easier. Less clutter means less to clean. Fewer commitments mean more time to relax and drink tea curled up next to the fire. Practically speaking, less means more.

Let me be clear. We have four kids, and we actually live in our home. We don't live in an HGTV show. My minivan is full of crumbs, spare coats, and shoes (so many shoes!). Our kitchen has dishes in the sink (likely from yesterday, but let's just ignore that and keep moving). Our laundry room has, you guessed it, dirty laundry! However messy and lived-in our home is thanks to our daily schedules, normal life, and raising small humans, our home **is easy to clean,** and everything has a place to go.

How did we get there? By creating guidelines for our family that make decisions very easy. The kids know where the shoes are supposed to go even if they don't make it there most of the time. I'm just as guilty as they are on this one, though. Each dish has a home once it's clean. The laundry will get sorted someday hopefully, but everyone knows where the basket is and which drawer their pjs go in. None of this happened immediately; it's taken years of working through systems, mindsets, and practices to cultivate. We started when our kids were little, so it was easier for us to integrate into our family's habits than it might be for someone who has older kids. This will always be a work in progress because we are human, and humans are messy. But as Jon likes to say, "You eat an elephant one bite at a time." So little by little we move forward.

Time to Get to Work

Before we jump headfirst into organizing a drawer or a space, let's talk about the process. Start by setting your goal for the space you're working in. This goal needs to be SMART (specific, measurable, achievable, relevant, and timely) and answer a precise question related to the space. The more detailed you can be with your goals, the easier it becomes to reach them. Instead of ' I want to clean out my junk drawer," put more specific parameters around your goal: "In one hour I want to have decluttered and reorganized the junk drawer of our kitchen by removing the excess pens and scrap paper while keeping the items that will be needed during regular life." Another example might be: "When I make lunches, I want to have a station that can streamline the process with easy access to all the supplies I need."

If it's helpful, you can find a way to display your goal while working or give yourself a phrase to repeat in your head to keep you on track if you get distracted. Along with your goal, ask yourself, "What could make this process easier?" and "How can I reduce my mental load when it comes to this space?" Using "When I . . ." statements is a great framework for understanding what you might need out of a particular location in your home. "When I open my linen closet, I want to find the spare sheets without having all the extra pillows fall on my head." The more direct you are with your goals, the easier it is to identify what needs to be edited, what can stay, and how the space should be organized.

Once you feel like you have a solid plan and goal in mind, you can get started. Always start small—and start with physical items. Your first project should not be a calendar overhaul or reorganizing all your kitchen cabinets. A simple drawer is a great place to begin. Pick your drawer and make sure it's a standalone project. My dad says projects are "slippery slopes" where one inevitably becomes more. A lot of times folks will try to start with a massive goal and then get tired midproject, leaving a huge mess and no desire to proceed. We already know this isn't an overnight fix, so starting small helps keep up the momentum for long-term progress.

So now you have your sights set on your one drawer. Maybe it's the kitchen junk drawer, your entryway table drawer, or even your bathroom drawer. No preference here for which drawer it is—just don't pick your pantry, a closet, or the playroom to begin with. Take everything out of the drawer. (Yes, everything.) As you take things out, categorize like items with like items (i.e., toothbrushes don't go in the same pile as moisturizers. Pens and tape go in separate piles. You get the point.) Once the drawer is completely empty, wipe it out. I bet it needs it. Next, tackle the piles. Remove anything broken, lost, or you have too many of. This is called *editing*, and it's likely the hardest part of the process when you're just getting started. You'll have to decide how many of a particular item is the right amount and what to do with the excess. Here's where it's helpful to have a plan for where you'll send donations, what your goal is for the space you are cleaning, and what your vision is once you've finished. My goal is always to be able to see everything inside a drawer. If I have to dig, then there's too much.

Once you've completed the editing, replace neatly only the right amount of whatever goes in that drawer. You can get bins or dividers to help keep things organized if you'd like, but sometimes it's easier to maintain without those. I often find them more stressful to maintain than just a big, empty drawer ready for something to be thrown in. Remember, we are parents, so we don't always have time for neatly folded dish towels. Sometimes we need to chug through our chores because we have five minutes until nap time is over and we needed to be at the bus stop thirty seconds ago. Empty drawers or shelves are good. Don't be pressured to fill space.

Whatever you do, don't rationalize keeping extra items for the sake of "I might need it someday." If something is really that important that you'll need it someday, you'll likely be able to acquire another. After you put everything back in your drawer, immediately take out the trash and move your donation pile out as soon as possible. Mistake number one is that we make all the progress on cleaning out a space and then let the last 1 percent of the job linger for too long. Donations and trash must go. My rule is that every time we order diapers, I have to fill the box from the last order with items to donate. I can't have two donation boxes going at one time (unless it's Christmas), so I need to get the donation box out before the next box is started. This is my system, but you can create your own way to help keep you motivated to get the donation and trash piles out of your house. If you've decided you don't need it, then don't keep it.

Do What Works

We are not living the lives my grandparents lived where there was a necessity to save every item we acquired. It's a blessing and a curse for sure. We are living a truly blessed life in that we don't have to worry about many things our grandparents and parents worried about, but there's also the burden of evolution. We are reshaping and relearning what works for our generation.

Most millennials are currently trending toward a life of less clutter because our parents and grandparents did not. Imagine your childhood home or your grandparent's home. I remember things being cozy, with piles everywhere, and lots of stuff I wasn't supposed to touch. A visit to Grandma and Grandpa's was often confusing because I loved going to see them but didn't understand why I wasn't allowed in certain rooms or why the pretty grapes were only for decoration. (Turns out they were fake grapes—ask me how I know.) My goal as a parent is to never have a home in which my kids can't live. If we have piles of things they shouldn't touch, that's a "me" problem, not a "them" problem. Our homes are meant to be where *all* family members find comfort. If we have parts of our house filled with items not meant to be touched or are being saved for later, who is benefitting from that clutter? Our kids certainly aren't. If anything, it's confusing for them and stressful for us. Move the donations out, and while you're at it, ditch the fake grapes too.

Editing takes mental fortitude and can be exhausting. Build yourself up to the harder larger tasks by thinking of editing as a muscle. It would be a massive mistake to hit the bench press at your one-rep max from ten years ago if you haven't lifted anything since then. You have to put in the work, starting with small weights until your body is ready to lift the heavy stuff. So go for the easier, smaller projects that will build you up for the bigger tasks. Saying "no" to an extra two dozen pens in your junk drawer is much easier than saying "no" to your great-aunt for Thanksgiving dinner.

LET'S CHOOSE LESS EDITING STEPS:

- ▶ Pick your space.
- ▶ Set your goal. (Be "SMART" and ask yourself "What is the purpose of this space?")
- ▶ Take everything out. (Don't forget to clean up the dust bunnies left behind!)
- ▶ Sort like items into piles.
- ▶ Edit excess, broken, or unneeded items.
- ▶ Return what is left to your space.
- ▶ Take out the trash and get donations out of the house ASAP.
- ▶ Repeat.

You'll be surprised by how easily this process becomes a habit. A drawer will turn into a cabinet, which might inspire you to tackle your closet or maybe even the playroom. Little by little, you'll make progress until one day you realize how much you've done and how much easier it is. The process of donating will get easier too. Your vision of what you want inside your home will become clearer. Your family may start to understand, and you'll make progress toward a lighter, less cluttered, less burdened you. But all your hard work decluttering and editing will be meaningless if you also don't change your purchasing habits.

Practice Mindful Purchasing

As you develop and strengthen your editing skills, you'll also need to begin practicing **mindful purchasing**. You can clean all you want, but if the number of things you are bringing into your home is greater than what is leaving, you aren't solving the problem. Imagine trying to build a sandcastle in the middle of a thunderstorm. All the progress you make toward a castle will be washed away by the rain or the tide, plus your castle won't have a solid foundation on which to stand.

Before you buy anything, you need to be sure it's something you need versus want and that it will have a place inside of your home immediately. Now that you are working toward a life of less, gone are the days where you impulse shop for something you think is pretty or might need another time. You shop with purpose. When you enter a store, you know exactly why you are there and go home with what is on your list.

Costco is our main source of grocery shopping, and it's also the easiest place to shop *without* purpose for us. We have a lot of mouths to feed, so buying our produce in bulk is necessary for our finances and for all the food we go through in a week. To get to the produce section in Costco requires walking to the very back of the store, past the home goods, electronics, the random dude trying to sell you a cell phone, the holiday décor, the clothing section, and my own personal kryptonite: office supplies. Then, if we need milk, we will need to walk to the other side of the store past all the baked goods, fancy cheese, the sample people, and the wine. By the time we get to the frozen section, our carts could easily be filled with things we don't need but look great on the shelf.

Stores are designed to pull our attention away from our lists and onto the shelves so we buy more. Stores want us to go home with a lot of stuff because it means more success for them. Stores and brands have no interest in helping us buy only what we need; they only want to make us spend more money than we intended when we entered. Product design and shelf marketing are strategically crafted to grab attention and make us believe we need to buy a certain product. Shopping with purpose means putting on blinders so we don't get distracted and instead can focus on our purpose for being in a store. If we buy everything that looks good from the front door of Costco to the dairy section, our cart, our car, and our house won't have any room for the milk we need.

Before we started on our journey to live more purposely and simply, Jon would never go shopping with me, and I couldn't understand why. "But it's so much fun just to browse and look!" was always my argument. I had a thing for decorative tchotchkes that would pile up on our small shelves, tabletops, and bookshelf (emphasis on the singular here because we only had room for one bookshelf). Our home was filled with clutter I found at home décor stores that

I thought was supposed to make our space feel like home. All it did was add to our stress levels. I thought we would solve the issues of our rented spaces not "feeling like home" by actually buying a home. But we had made ourselves a home a long time before, and I just wasn't aware of it. I had been conditioned to believe that since my rental townhouse, apartment, or first home didn't look like the pages of a magazine, I needed to buy better decor to make it more "homey" or beautiful. But "home" isn't about the décor—it's about the people inside. Once I understood that my impulsive, shelf-filling shopping habits were only hurting our home environment and our finances, I started to view shopping differently.

Mindful purchasing isn't about avoiding shopping, just like essentialism and minimalism aren't about owning nothing. It's about being aware of what we spend our money on and what comes into our homes. Each time you go shopping, try to have a list and a reason for why you're entering a store. Better yet, online shopping (even for small businesses) can be helpful because you remove a lot of the external marketing stimulation stores have.

The goal of shopping purposefully is to only buy what you need. Imagine going to the mall and leaving with just a few items—or even with nothing. When you shop mindfully, you're thinking beyond the doors of the store. You're planning where this particular item will go in your home and deciding whether you have too many duplicates of it already. You're thinking about what you might need to donate to bring this item home, or if it's actually something you need. This is *really* hard but absolutely necessary if you want to make progress toward living a life of less. You can't quit your job as a "stuff manager" if you are still bringing stuff home faster than you are getting rid of things.

If you get rid of all your clutter but don't know *why* you're doing it, there's no point. Knowing the reasons behind why you want to live a life of less is more important than having a lovely-looking linen closet. You can have the world's most organized, clutter-free home, but if you and your family aren't solid in your shared mission, you will inevitably lose your way.

 ## *LET'S CHOOSE LESS* DOS:

- ▶ Choose to lose. Start with losing all the excess so you can start winning.
- ▶ Start with a small project.
- ▶ Prioritize quality items over quantity.
- ▶ Shop with a mission to only bring home what you need.
- ▶ Keep your family mission statement in mind when organizing or shopping.

LET'S CHOOSE *LESS* DON'TS:

- ▶ Don't feel obligated to use bins with every organizing project.
- ▶ Don't let the donation or trash pile sit.
- ▶ Don't be afraid when someone questions you.
- ▶ Don't have fake grapes for decorations.
- ▶ Don't buy something on impulse.
- ▶ Don't enter a store without a plan.

Journal Prompt/Discussion Questions:

What was your childhood home like?

Is there something you'd like to replicate or avoid from those childhood experiences in your home?

What is scaring you about this process so far?

What are you most excited about?

PART TWO

LET'S CHOOSE LESS
IN OUR HOME

CHAPTER 4

HOME SWEET HOME

If you have the space, you will fill it.

W e purchased our next home in 2021 on a whim. Jon and I were torn about whether we should renovate the house we had been living in or move somewhere new. While I was looking for houses, he was thinking up renovation plans until I stumbled upon a listing three-quarters of a mile from my childhood home. It took about five minutes from the moment I walked in until I was calling Jon at home to come see it. We had found our forever home, and it happened to be the ugliest house in the neighborhood. The only reason we were able to buy it was that no one else wanted her. (Yes, she's a "she.") Our "new to us" house is an old gal who needs a lot of love but has the best view, a lot of wallpaper, solid bones, and feels just like home.

The moment we signed the deed (this time I was right about needing to sign a deed), we began renovating, and we haven't stopped yet. If you name a part of a house, we have either replaced it already or plan to at some point. This place has been a definite labor of love. On the hard days, we've joked that it might have been easier to just knock it down and start over, but so far, we haven't resorted to that option. Each completed project brings such a sense of pride in how hard we've worked or what we've endured (like moving out for more than a week to replace all the ductwork) to accomplish something in our home. She's a work in progress.

When you walk in, you're greeted with partially painted trim, some rooms finished, and others not. Kids' art is taped to the walls in almost every room. There are random holes in the walls and bathrooms with wallpaper from the 1980s peeling off. Projects are all around us, yet this house feels like a true home—a space where we can actually *live*. Our goal isn't to have a magazine-perfect home (although let's be real, that would be kinda great). But four kids do not equal an HGTV-worthy house . . . ever. The goal for our home is to make people feel comfortable.

Our space has a clearly defined purpose: **to be somewhere kids and grownups can live**. Toys are usually scattered all over. You'll likely find a child's outfit strewn about a hallway where they decided to disrobe and walk away. The kitchen is always open, even if I don't want it to be. It's not the end of the world if you accidentally pull a tassel off a throw pillow (seriously, it's just a pillow). We live here, and it feels like it. When friends come over, the last thing I want is for them to apologize when their kids pull a toy off the shelf or get crumbs on the floor. (Although I do detest crumbs, they are a part of life.) Homes are meant to be lived in, and ours most certainly is.

But this wasn't always the case.

There was a time when I was more concerned with my vignettes of tchotchkes and home décor than how our space made people feel. Everything needed to be coiffed just so and look a certain way to keep up with the unreasonable standards my brain had set for our home. It was exhausting and increasingly unrealistic with each kid we had. Over the years, I have learned that being a parent is just one long lesson in relinquishing control in every aspect of your life, especially in having a "perfect" home.

Nowadays our décor has purpose and makes sense for everyone who lives under our roof. Breakable décor doesn't exist in our house. Books fill our shelves, so when we want to share a great one with a friend we know right where to find it. Toys are in our sunroom where moms can drink coffee and kids can play. The dining room (which you'll learn more about soon) is the most kid-friendly room in the house. Our home is not the prettiest, but I guarantee you'll feel like you can easily settle in on the couch.

Room to Breathe

When you know what the purpose of your space is, editing out the clutter is a piece of cake. Maybe you agree that stacks of lovely décor don't add to your environment but rather detract from what you're trying to achieve in your home. We want those who walk through our doors to feel like family. So the people are the priority, not the things.

When we began our editing journey, décor was one of the largest areas of donations for me, but it wasn't where we began. I wasn't brave enough yet. Jon and I started our journey with the physical things we could see and control like toys, our closets, the kitchen, and sentimental items. It's funny in hindsight that I was able to get rid of sentimental items from my childhood more easily than my precious home furnishings. We tend to place our attention on the wrong things—and for me, it was cute décor for the beautiful home I had envisioned.

As we emptied bins and made room, I realized how much I love empty space in a house. I wanted more space, so the décor had to go. It was easier to say no once I realized what I was saying yes to instead. Room to breathe and move was more important to me than a cute display. **As I got rid of things, our house became more beautiful to me.** Never could I have imagined that less stuff would mean more beauty. We still have a long way to go. Projects are everywhere — including editing projects—but as long as we keep moving forward with the expectation that our home isn't meant to be perfect, we are doing just fine.

The Playroom Pare Down

Every area of a home benefits from *Let's Choose Less*. For us, our playroom was the easiest and most necessary location to begin our editing process. We didn't follow our own advice of "starting small." (We also didn't have the sage advice of our future selves to tell us where it was easiest to start!) Speaking from experience: please don't make the same mistakes we did! Let it be known that it is *always* easier to get rid of someone else's things than your own, especially annoying kids' toys. But this was not our intention. Our goal was to regain some control over a major eyesore, source of stress, and problem area of our home.

Back when we were still squished in our sweet little two-bedroom townhouse with just Emily (aka the wonder baby who needed no sleep ever), I was telling Jon that there were toys everywhere. I felt like all I was doing all day long was cleaning up toys. We didn't have a dedicated playroom, so play time either happened in our living room or Emily's bedroom. If we wanted space to walk, we had to clean up after every play session just to get from one end of the room to the other. I would clean up as she played because I knew that if I let things progress on their own, it would take me forever to tidy up, and I needed to tidy up if we wanted to make it through the living room to get to the kitchen for lunch. I was newly pregnant, so lunch was really important.

In my complaints to Jon, I kept asking, "How in the world can we make this easier?" because I was tired of cleaning up so many stuffed animals, toys that make noise, and little tiny pieces. Jon kindly suggested a toy rotation plus maybe getting rid of a few things. I told him he was crazy. There was no way I was going to deprive my sweet baby of her one thousand very necessary, very noisy, very messy, very annoying collection of every toy she owned. Yeah, that idea got turned down faster than a bowl of Cheerios falling from a high chair. This went on for years. Jon would sweetly suggest something similar, and I would flat-out refuse.

Jon and I were introduced to Montessori education when we read the book *Montessori Toddler: A Parent's Guide to Raising a Curious and Responsible Human Being* by Simone Davies. Dr. Maria Montessori was a female doctor in the 1800s who took care of poor and sick children in Rome. She used her medical training to apply a science-based approach to help children learn. Thus she created the Montessori education method and has influenced education models all over the world. Montessori learning utilizes a dynamic, individualized relationship between teacher, student, and learning environment. The objective of Montessori education is "to not fill a child with facts, but to cultivate their own desire to learn."[10] Montessori principles encompass all aspects of a child's life, not just time in a classroom. The entire world is a child's classroom with Montessori, and everyday activities are part of their education. A major lesson we learned from Dr. Montessori was to utilize a toy rotation (yes, Jon was right) and to pick open-ended toys (toys that can be played with in a number of ways, not single purpose).

Let's Choose Less is a well-balanced array of concepts, so we don't utilize only Montessori ideas in our play spaces, but it does inform us on how we set up our home to encourage

---

10 Simone Davies, *The Montessori Toddler: A Parent's Guide to Raising a Curious and Responsible Human Being* (New York: Workman Publishing, 2019), 14.

open-ended, educational, and fun play for our kids. Montessori gave us a road map to understand our kids. Once we knew
why they were doing the same activity over and over, or why
the flashy, loud toys weren't being used as often, we were able
to curate their play space and toy selections to make their
time more efficient and fun. We immediately set to work on
getting battery-powered, single-use toys out of the way so our
kids had the time and ability to focus. Hence the reason we
started in the playroom. We had a clear mission and vision.
Our playroom had a purpose.

Here's an unpopular opinion: don't have a playroom.
GASP. Did she just say that? Yep, I did. When we were in our
tiny townhome, we were covered in toys (plus all the other
junk too), but we were forced to limit the number of toys we
owned based on the space we had. If you have space, you'll
likely fill it. If you have a huge playroom, you're likely to fill
it up with toys.

In our first house, we had an entire basement for
a playroom. It was ridiculous how much space our kids had for
toys. And do you know where they played? In our living room
or outside. The playroom was pointless. Kids will gravitate
toward where everyone else is, so if you have a playroom off
on its own, you'll likely still find your kid at your feet playing
on the kitchen floor while you try to make dinner.

If you have the gift of a dedicated playroom, I challenge
you to leave most of it empty or fill it with a larger play
item like a Pickler Climbing Gym, a Nugget Play Couch,
a climbing wall, or a sensory swing. Most kids would rather

have room to move than small items intended to entertain them. There's nothing wrong with open space in our homes. In the back of this book, you'll find a resource section with gift ideas for each age group to help thoughtfully curate an open-ended, fun space for kids in your home.

Our current home doesn't have a playroom, and we don't miss it at all. We have a dedicated corner of our sunroom where kids' toys and books live, plus a fun mini-climbing gym that is constantly used. Our kids have a handful of toys in their bedrooms, but it's rare to find them playing there. As you set up your play space, whether it's a full-size playroom or just a small corner in your living room, keep your family's personalities in mind and then design your space accordingly. If you love to read, you might have books and bookshelves everywhere.

Other helpful tools to keep the number of toys in your home to a minimum include a toy and book rotation, prioritizing the right kinds of toys for your kids' ages and your family's lifestyle, and open shelving. The more places you can hide things, the easier it is to lose items in the abyss of space.

▶ **Utilize toy rotation:** Just because you only display a few things to play with at any given time doesn't mean you need to throw all the other toys away. Unless you have completely run out of extra storage space—in which case you'll then need to do some editing. Keep most of the toys out of reach and rotate them out every so often. You can have fun with your rotations and create themes for your setups. Rotating also keeps your kids' toys exciting and new. You'd be amazed at what kids can forget about and how excited they get to see an old friend again. We keep one big bin of toys out of rotation and a box in the attic of books that are rotated in and out. Everything is easily switched, and we do it on a time interval that works for us. If the kids are really into something, it may stay out longer than something that's not getting much attention.

▶ **Prioritize open-ended toys:** Toys come in all kinds of categories, and we have found that ones with batteries are not lengthy attention grabbers. If we are buying our kids a toy, we look for open-ended and non-battery-powered. If we are given a toy with batteries, we won't refuse it, but the batteries will not get replaced once they wear out. We keep educational toys or activities easily accessible.

▶ **Employ open shelving:** I borrowed this one straight from the Montessori handbook, and it works wonderfully. If you can see all the toys you have out, your kids will be able to find what they are looking for easily. It prevents the inevitable "bottom of the basket" toys that seem to linger and get lost. If there's no room for you to keep pushing something to the bottom of the basket, then you must choose what stays or goes. It also makes cleaning up very simple because things must make it back into their spot on the shelf instead of being sorted into a particular bin or basket.

When Guests Come to Play

Sometimes a friend's child will ask, "Where are the rest of the toys?"—or my favorite: "You don't have very many things to play with." I answer that on both accounts, they are correct. This was a major fear of mine, but it hasn't been a major issue, and it's been a great conversation starter with friends. The toys that are out of rotation are never far away, so we can pull out extra activities if we need to, but we rarely have to. Kids are wildly creative and don't need much to play, but parents often feel obligated to provide them with far more options than they need. When our kids have friends over, the kids get so busy with something—like making their own costumes from construction paper—that they hardly think to ask where more toys are because they are having too much fun to care. We also play outside a lot, and that requires little to no toys at all!

Death by Decisions

Remember, *Let's Choose Less* is different for everyone. It doesn't mean having nothing; it's just pursuing fewer things instead of more. Having only the essentials in your play space offers less clutter, more opportunity for focused play, and more room for imagination. If there's one reason to have a play space with only the essentials and utilizing a toy rotation, I would say it's to fight all the different kinds of fatigue: decision fatigue for kids while they play, the fatigue of repeatedly cleaning up the same things for parents, and the fatigue of maintaining too many items for everyone. Have you ever watched a kid dump out an entire toy basket only to find one thing, play for a minute, and then move on while leaving the mess behind them? This is a child exhibiting decision fatigue.

Decision fatigue can appear in many different forms for kids. It might be a lack of control (maybe dumping out all the toys), a meltdown, an inability to make choices (looking at a big pile of toys but saying they have nothing to play with), irritability, or even impulsivity. No matter how it manifests, decision fatigue usually results in a negative outcome. Many parents of older children can easily identify this during the after-school emotional breakdown. A child has spent their entire school day trying to make decisions, and then they emotionally crumble when arriving home to a safe space. Decision fatigue can come from within your home as well, particularly in the playroom.

If a child has too many options in front of them, they can't sift through them all easily, so they move on. It is similar to how a grown-up would feel shopping for something only to find too many options and feel overwhelmed trying to figure out which one to choose. Jon and I took three years to buy a mattress one time because we simply couldn't decide which one to get. By eliminating too many choices and offering fewer decisions in the playroom, kids can focus for longer and receive greater benefits from the toy options given. I noticed this when Emily and Sophie were around the ages of four and three, before we began editing and rotating toys. The girls would raid our puzzle cabinet and dump every single puzzle out, mix all the pieces together, and then move on to playing with something else instead. I have pictures of our lovely formal living room covered in small pieces from dozens of puzzle boxes, and it gives me hives just thinking about it. We would spend hours getting it all back to where it belonged just to have the process repeat the next day. I started locking the cabinet to "break them of the habit," but in reality, it was just as overwhelming for them as it was for me. Their little brains were fatigued with all the options and they couldn't decide, so they would just dump it all out and focus on something else. Sounds a little like me in the aisle of HomeGoods during the Christmas season, except I tend to leave all the items on the shelf so I don't have to pay for them all. Once we started doing a toy rotation and only had a few puzzles available at a time, they would play for hours. Emily and Sophie *love* puzzles now, but I don't think they would if we hadn't pared down on the options so there was more freedom to choose and enjoy a little at a time.

Less Time to Clean Up!

Along with the decision-making benefits, having a minimal toy setup also means less to clean up! We all know it's inevitable that kids will make messes if they can, but when there's less to clean it's not as big of a deal when the playroom gets messy. And I will be honest that our play area can still get *really* messy.

As we progress in this book, we will cover maternity supplies, baby gear, things toddlers love, and lots of other fun stuff, but if there's one place every home could use *Let's Choose Less*, it's the playroom. If you haven't gotten to the "playroom stage" of parenting yet, knowing these principles now will make a massive difference in preparing your home for kids. Play is a child's job, so having the right supplies and the right setup can make play more enjoyable for everyone.

 ## A TYPICAL PLAY SPACE FOR YOUNGER KIDS AGES TWO AND THREE:

- ▶ Bookshelf with twelve to fifteen seasonal or themed books
- ▶ A basket of DUPLO® or wooden building blocks
- ▶ A play basketball goal with several small basketballs
- ▶ Three to five toy trucks
- ▶ One to two baby dolls
- ▶ Dress-up clothes kept in a storage ottoman
- ▶ Indoor playset

Journal Prompts/Discussion Questions:

▶ What area of your home would be most impacted by a clean-out?

▶ Is a playroom necessary in your house?

▶ Do you remember any favorite toys from your childhood?

▶ Are there toys in your home currently that don't have a designated spot to return to?

▶ Is there a common room in your home where kids could play instead of a playroom?

CHAPTER 5

REIMAGINING EATING SPACES

Rooms with purpose.

Dining Room—Or Art Studio?

We are not formal people. We've never hosted a fancy dinner party, and I wish we had never registered for our formal dining china at our wedding. (Sorry, Mom.) A formal dining room is a completely unnecessary space for us.

For a long time, our dining room was one giant storage room. It was home for all the stuff that didn't have a home, and it drove me crazy. I would purposely avoid walking through it just so I didn't have to experience that gut-sinking feeling when I saw all the unpacked boxes, the random stroller, extra folding chairs, and anything else we didn't know what to do with. (Yes, we kept a stroller in our dining room for months for no reason other than we might need it someday.)

Then one day our whole family got sick. You know the deal. One kid would be sick for a week then get better, and the next day another kid would be sick. It was the *worst*, and we were all stuck at home for way longer than any of us wanted to be. I kept trying to come up with new activities for the healthy kids to stay entertained and quiet while the sick kids rested, but I was quickly running out of ideas. So I used some old baby gates to cordon off the dining room and pushed all the junk to one side to clear a space. I set up a massive sensory bin station, and my kids played for *hours*. Suddenly, our useless dining room wasn't so useless. It had new purpose, and I was determined to bring my vision to life.

Our kids love to color, do messy projects, crafts, and paint, but every time they would get spread out at the kitchen table, we would have to clean it up in time for the next meal. Enter the repurposed dining room. Everything had to go. The stroller was finally sold, the boxes unpacked, and I purchased a cheap and very ugly dining room table and chairs set for sale on Facebook Marketplace. An old rug went under the ugly chairs, and voila, our dining room had a new mission: the ideal kid's art room.

Having space for our kids to create freely has been revolutionary in their ability to entertain themselves, in my ability to let go of arts and crafts messes, and in giving new life to a rarely used space. We store art supplies in a coat closet by our front door or in an old dresser within arm's reach of the little artists sitting at the table. The table itself has marks, glue, paint, and who knows what else on it, and I don't care!

Seriously, it was in rough shape before our kids got to it so in some ways, I think their artistic touches have improved the aesthetic. Our kids can run in whenever they want to color for a few minutes or hours. The reactions of friends who walk in and see a room filled with our kids' art is priceless, and there's plenty of room for extra kids to join in.

We have since become a homeschool family, and our dining room is now also our schoolroom as well. The walls are covered in art up to the ceiling. As a masterpiece is finished, the kids are allowed to pick out a space for it to hang on the walls, which feels like a total cool mom flex to me. I was never allowed to tape things on the walls growing up, so now the benefits of our old, unfinished home projects come full circle. Is it the dining room you'll find in the pages of *Southern Living* magazine? Absolutely not. But the room has a purpose, and it serves our family well. We turned a room from hardly used to being the most popular place in our house with the addition of some ugly furniture and a new mindset. The best part is that I didn't have to do any of the decorating.

Kitchen Chronicles

The kitchen in our old house was just right for us. We had the perfect amount of cabinet space, just enough room for the kids to sit at the counter to eat, and everything close at hand, making clean up easy. The kitchen in our current house could use some love (surprise, surprise). Imagine a kitchen that was fashionable in the 1980s but now . . . not so much. Dark cabinets, dark countertops, appliances from the '80s, and wallpaper with pears on it. It's definitely got some character, and we have no plans for changing it anytime soon. I've actually come to adore the garish wallpaper, and the dark countertops hide messes wonderfully well.

The worst part of our kitchen is that not a single shelf in the cabinets can be adjusted. This means our kitchen is one giant puzzle, and it takes some serious math to figure out where and how to store things. When we moved in, the kitchen forced us to evaluate every item going into the cabinets because many things we owned wouldn't fit. We have plenty of empty shelves because none of our water bottles, serving ware, or Tupperware can fit on them! When your space can't accommodate the things you own, it's a good reason to evaluate the necessity of all those things. We didn't need all the water bottles we were trying to fit, so we pared down to a more reasonable number that could be turned on their sides to be stored. We decanted a lot of our dry goods into beautiful glass jars to be displayed on a shelf in our kitchen instead of shoving Tupperware into whatever space we could find. Serving pieces are used as decor on living room shelves, and it looks great!

A huge kitchen storage obstacle for us was all the kid-related kitchen items we owned. Plastic plates, kid-size forks, sippy cups, and bottle supplies can easily overcome any space. The rule of thumb for us is that everyone in our family has enough of something for a day—two sippy cups, a plate for each meal, a fork for each meal, etc. We run our dishwasher most evenings, so unless something major happens, we typically have plenty of what we need. We keep a small amount over our base number to accommodate guests comfortably, for inevitable spills, or for things that break, but you won't find a stack of twenty sippy cups inside of our fabulously unique cabinets. We also have a drawer with diner baskets and parchment paper for nonmessy meals. Instead of always dirtying a dish, we will grab a basket for a quick sandwich lunch or a handful of crackers. It leaves dishes for when they are needed, and the kids can clean up after themselves easily.

Sometimes our spaces require us to look at things from a different angle. Instead of renovating the kitchen as soon as we moved in, we decided to find a functional alternative such as paring down on excess or finding innovative storage ideas like using serving ware as decor—and the results have worked well.

Journal Prompts/Discussion Questions:

▶ What is your home's purpose?

▶ Do you have other rooms that could serve better purposes?

▶ Where do you spend the most time in your home?

▶ Are there any empty cabinets in your kitchen?

CHAPTER 6

CLOSETS AND CAPSULE WARDROBES

Don't be a Monica.

One of my all-time favorite TV shows is *Friends*. I'm Monica and not afraid to admit it. I love a tidy space, I usually have a system for everything, and I find great joy in cleaning. The biggest difference between me and Monica is our closets. There's an episode (Season 8, Episode 14 to be exact) when everyone discovers Monica has a secret closet overflowing with junk that she keeps behind a locked door. Her friends open the door and are shocked by the mess. Our goal with *Let's Choose Less* is to avoid having a "Monica closet." The average home in America has approximately 300,000 items in it at any given time, and the average home size in America has tripled in the last fifty years.[11] Homes

---

11 Joshua Becker, "21 Surprising Statistics That Reveal How Much Stuff We Actually Own," Becoming Minimalist, https://www.becomingminimalist.com/clutter-stats.

have more space than ever, yet somehow we are running out of room to store things. A tidy house with overflowing closets is the same as cleaning your floors by sweeping all the dust under your rug. It may help in the short term by eliminating visual clutter, but eventually you'll have to deal with it.

The Closet Clean Out

For a room to be declared a bedroom, it must include three things: a window, a door, and a closet. If we follow that line of thought hypothetically, every bedroom in America has a closet, and a typical American household has at least two other closets not located in a bedroom. That's a lot of closet space to keep tidy—and a lot of stuff to keep track of! Closets come in all shapes and sizes, but one thing most of them have in common is that they get filled to the brim. What if we changed that story and had room to spare in every closet in our home? What if you opened the door and could not only see the floor but also the back of the closet and were able to locate exactly what you were looking for quickly? Sounds dreamy, right? It's absolutely possible. Welcome to step one: the closet clean out.

Whether it's your linen closet, your pantry, your bedroom closet, or a hall closet, you can follow the same steps. The process is pretty similar to the editing steps we covered earlier. Take everything out of the closet. Pile it all on the bed, the floor, or that random chair in the corner of your room. Next, sort everything into piles. If I'm doing clothes, I usually do a dress pile, a sweater pile, pants, shirts, etc. (It helps to do this *as* you take everything out!) Get rid of anything that hasn't been used or worn in a long time, doesn't fit, isn't from this decade, is completely out of style, or is covered in dust. Identify what you want to go back into your closet and determine the easiest way to access everything within the closet. You don't have to get rid of everything; just concentrate on getting rid of what you don't need and focus on what you need the most. Remember, less is more!

 ## LET'S CHOOSE LESS CLOSET CLEANING STEPS:

- ▶ Remove everything from your closet and drawers.
- ▶ Sort like items into piles (seasons, types of clothes, sizing, life stage).
- ▶ Edit excess, items with holes or tears, unneeded items, anything from the 1990s, or anything that doesn't fit.
- ▶ Return the rest to your space.
- ▶ Remove donations and trash.
- ▶ Repeat.

Closet cleaning is far easier for Jon than for me. I feel the social pressure as a woman to have different outfits for different circumstances and occasions plus multiple sizes thanks to the postpartum/pregnancy roller coaster. Jon, on the other hand, is a champ at getting rid of all the "back of the drawer," "don't wear it ever," and "never going to need it again" stuff. He basically transformed his wardrobe in a day, and it's taken me years to catch up. Part of the challenge was that I was pregnant or nursing over those years and couldn't get rid of as much as I wanted to because I couldn't fit into half of what I owned at any given point. So I started looking into capsule wardrobes, and I discovered that I had accidentally created multiple capsule wardrobes for myself years ago.

What is a capsule wardrobe?

A capsule wardrobe is a small, curated collection of clothes that may have a common color palette to be mixed and matched for a particular season. Think "fall capsule wardrobe" with tans and dark neutrals that can be interchanged with a few pairs of boots or jackets for different looks. Typically, most women use it for a weather season, but I found I was also using it for a "season of life": maternity clothes, postpartum clothes, nursing-friendly clothes, and regular clothes. I was way ahead in the capsule wardrobe game before I even realized it!

At first, it can seem like a scary thing to do because you are taking so much out and only leaving a certain number of pieces, but the best part is that you don't have to adhere to any rules. I started with "seasons of life," but you could start with just a regular weather season. Take out all your clothes for a particular season and play a game of how many different outfit combinations you can make with only a small number of your clothing items. You can also identify if any major important pieces are missing in your wardrobe (I realized a few years ago that I had several pairs of jeans but not even one fit me), or see if you can replace multiple pieces of just "OK" clothes with one or two high-quality pieces instead. Remember my yoga pants? We are talking about the essentials, people. This is a great opportunity to pare down in numbers and concentrate on quality.

Can I do this for my kids' clothes?

You sure can. I started doing this for our kids when I was trying to convince my independent, second born, Sophie, that winter clothes are not for summer and Jon made the statement, "Why not just put away the options you don't want her to pick from?" (He's a smart guy.) So, all the kids' winter and fall clothes are not in their closets and drawers until the weather starts to turn a little chilly. As the seasons change, so do their wardrobes and usually the sizes of their clothes. This helps me feel like we aren't drowning in multiple sizes and multiple seasons of clothes in every closet. Each season I do a closet refresh—things that are too small get handed down, anything that isn't appropriate for the season gets put away, clothes that are worn out are recycled or donated, and new sizes of clothes are added to fill in any missing gaps.

How do I start a capsule wardrobe?

The hardest part is taking everything out of your closet. You don't have to completely pack away the clothes you aren't wearing each season if that adds to your stress level, or if you don't have a separate space to store it. Just cordon off a portion of your closet as your active section and let the items you're not using make their way to the farther back spots in your closet. If you don't have enough wiggle room in your closet or dressers, it's time to look at what needs to be edited from your wardrobe.

It seems counterintuitive, but taking away all the excess options in my closet has opened me up to new wardrobe choices I wouldn't have noticed before. I love the simplicity of having less in front of me and the ease of not having decision fatigue over what to wear every day. I can grab the pieces I know will fit and look good without having to put myself through the "nothing fits" or "I have nothing to wear" battles because I know it all works. And if something doesn't work? Goodbye! No point in keeping it if it's no longer helping you or is adding stress to your life. As a busy mom, there's no time for that.

Remember, space is rarely the issue—too much stuff is. Only the essentials are what we need; everything else is just excess. A mess is never a bad thing, especially when you live with kids, but if you feel like you need to hide your mess behind a locked closet door, it's probably a good idea to address it.

Journal Prompts/Discussion Questions:

▶ Have you ever considered a capsule wardrobe?

▶ Do you have any clothing in your closet older than your marriage or kids?

▶ Is there one particular kind of clothing item you have an excess of?

▶ Is there a closet like Monica's in your home?

▶ How much is enough when it comes to closets?

CHAPTER 7

SENTIMENTAL ITEMS

Things can be replaced.

S entimental items undoubtedly fill most attics in America right alongside all the holiday decorations— so much so that we've had to create more space to store our belongings outside of our homes, leading to a significant boom in the storage industry. The self-storage industry boasts almost $40 billion in revenue each year. For scale, the total number of U.S. self-storage businesses as of February 2024 is around 50,523, more than the combined number of Starbucks, McDonald's, Dunkin' Donuts, Pizza Hut, and Wendy's restaurants across the United States. In 2018 there were estimated to be around 23,400,000 self-storage units for rent in the United States, which would equate to fourteen people per storage unit based on the U.S population at the time. Americans live in a consumer mindset, where we justify keeping something based on our ability to store it even if that item no longer serves a purpose. We are very talented at adding sentimental value to almost anything and rationalizing keeping an item even if it makes no sense. When we have kids, we take this to the extreme.[12]

Sentimental items are often the most challenging area of any home to edit. Why? Because these items are intertwined with our emotions. Memories attach themselves to things, and that's how they become sentimental. It isn't the doll we pick up from our memory bin and hold in our hands but the memory of playing with it for hours when we were little or the feeling when we opened the box for the first time. When our emotions are involved, our logic takes a back seat. This is what makes it difficult to clear our memory bins and significantly increases the challenge of deciding what to preserve for our children.

What to Save and What to Discard

There's no right way to determine how much or what kind of sentimental stuff is the appropriate amount to save. I could tell you a made-up formula, but the honest answer is that only you can decide that threshold. My opinions on what to save vary greatly from my mom's, my best friend's, and likely yours. We are all different; therefore, it would be unfair for me to write out a specific prescription for what you can and can't keep. You will have to figure that out for yourself, but

---

12 Colton Gardner, "Self Storage Industry Statistics (2024)," October 22, 2024, *Neighbor Blog*, https://www.neighbor.com/storage-blog/self-storage-industry-statistics/#supply.

if you need to rent a storage unit to store your sentimental items, it might be time to pare down.

Before you open a single bin, pull out an old math test, or read a long-lost love note from middle school, remember that emotions will be tied to this process. When you are aware of how these items make you feel, you will be able to more clearly decide what to do with them. Always make sure the items you choose to keep are associated with happy memories and fit within your family's value system. Jon and I give each of our kids a book for each holiday or birthday, often with a message written inside. As a family who highly values reading, these are precious, sentimental items for us. A toy that we picked up in a Chick-fil-A kids' meal isn't high on our "to be saved list." When you know what is important to your family, it takes the edge off that gut punch you feel when you discard something you feel obligated to save but have no reason to save.

Along with acknowledging how a particular item may make you feel, be sure it is in good enough condition to be saved. Some items don't stand the test of time no matter how badly we want them to. If something is damaged, rotted, or has the potential to create a mess, it might be best to let it go. I never knew that rubber bands could rot until I was peeling decades old rubber off of stacks of papers that had melted in the attic. Trust me, rubber can melt, and it gets gross once it does. Baby clothes with elastic in them will crack and dry rot, so sometimes those adorable outfits get ruined even with the best intentions of saving them forever. It goes without saying that anything a bug might find yummy is probably not something we should save long term. A lot of times the decision is made for us based on what the item is and it's longevity in our storage space.

Being a parent doesn't mean we need to save every item our child touches just in case they want it someday. Art projects can add up into the thousands, and if we saved every single one, our house might fall over with the weight of them all. I *always* save anything with a handprint or a thumbprint. I save the first time they write their names, the first face they draw that looks like a face, the notes that make me cry or laugh, and the monumental projects. Every coloring book page or scrap of paper they cut doesn't need to make it into that pile. When you save the truly important things, those things become even more precious.

A few questions to ask yourself while sifting through sentimental items that might make the process a little easier:

- ▶ If this is something from your childhood: does this remind me of a happy memory?
- ▶ Do we have room to store this?
- ▶ Are there duplicates of this item that I have already saved?
- ▶ What do I enjoy looking at from my childhood, and would my children like the same thing?
- ▶ Is this item still in good condition? Could it be repurposed for play or display?
- ▶ Will bugs want to eat this?

Where to Put the Saved Items

On one of my many editing attempts for my own childhood possessions, I came across my kindergarten backpack. Emily at the time was "helping" me go through things, and the backpack immediately caught her eye. My first reaction was to tell her not to touch and to return the backpack to the bin, but after watching her eyes light up over it, I realized this bag might serve a new purpose. Instead of keeping it locked in a bin, my hot pink, embroidered backpack has been used in countless hours of play over the years.

When Jon's grandma died, we learned she had been an avid teacup collector, and we inherited a dozen from her almost fifty unique teacups. At first, I kept them in a box locked away, but after encouragement from my mother-in-law, we have several on display around our house, and the rest have been used for formal tea parties with guests or to pass the time on sick days. Grandma Shirley is probably thrilled to see her great-grandkids enjoying something she loved so much. Not all sentimental items need to be stored away to be appreciated.

As wonderful as it would be to have a house full of your most precious memories on display, realistically most of your sentimental items will need to be stored somewhere. Before you pack up any boxes or reorganize your attic, have a clear idea of what kind of system you'd like to have in place for saving things. When it comes to my personal keepsakes, I keep them all in one bin in our attic. As the bin becomes too full,

I make it a priority to reedit to make room. For small little notes or special invitations, I tuck those into my journals.

Each of our kids has their own memory bin in their closet where all their keepsakes go. For each calendar year, I make each child a labeled zippered pouch in which all their important documents/notes/art/birthday cards/special items can be stored. If it doesn't fit in the pouch, it better be majorly important to be saved. At the end of each year, I transition everything to their memory bins. If the bin fills up, we need to look and see what's been saved that doesn't need to be. I've also heard of people buying premade, prelabeled file bins with a file folder for each year of your child's life, which probably makes school, art, and paper memory organization a breeze. If you're looking for the inspiration to help you cultivate the right level of sentimental items for your kids, go through your childhood sentimental items. If you get rid of it from your collection of saved items, don't save something similar for your kids.

Whenever someone loses something or breaks something in our house, we repeat the same mantra: "Things can be replaced." If you truly value something you remove from your house, you can always replace it if you want to. Things aren't what make your home feel like home; your family is. The items you touch and use on a daily, weekly, or monthly basis are the essentials. If it has dust on it, it's not essential. As *Let's Choose Less* becomes a natural part of your habits, you'll notice how much you must cull to find the good things to save. Skimming off the layers of unnecessary stuff frees your time and mental capacity to be more present, more relaxed, and less worried about things that truly don't have value.

 ## *LET'S CHOOSE LESS* TIPS FOR YOUR HOME:

- ▶ Identify the purpose of your home.
- ▶ Don't be afraid to ditch the playroom or dining room.
- ▶ Your toys are not the reason your visitors are visiting.
- ▶ Utilize a toy rotation, prioritize open-ended toys, and employ open shelving in the playroom.
- ▶ Use capsule wardrobes.
- ▶ Don't save something for your kids that you wouldn't want saved for you.

Journal Prompts/Discussion Questions:

- ▶ What is something sentimental that you saved from your childhood that you don't think is necessary to save for your kids?
- ▶ Do you have a favorite item from your childhood that you could share with your children?
- ▶ What is the most random or odd item you've saved for sentimental purposes?

PART THREE

LET'S CHOOSE LESS
FOR OUR FAMILY

CHAPTER 8

PREGNANCY AND POSTPARTUM

It's a wild ride.

Unpopular opinion: pregnancy is not my favorite. The ability to biologically create children is a gift I'm fully aware of and grateful for, but as someone who is very active, it was a hard time for me. Add the fact that I had four babies in five years, so there were years that I was pregnant more than I wasn't, and you might understand why it wasn't my best-loved season of life. Funny enough, I love birthing babies and I love babies—just not the pregnancy part of the process.

Pregnancy became a time of survival. It was a daily ritual to count down how many days were left until my due date and then roll those numbers around into different iterations to make it feel sooner than it likely was. Food was vital for keeping me alive but not really enjoyed thanks to nausea and reflux. Clothes were necessary because it's socially unacceptable to not wear them, but I wasn't looking in the mirror for the cute factor. Anything that could be turned into a survival tool for me had new meaning. Ice was life. Outfit repeating wasn't taboo in the least. I found my favorites and stuck to them, and it worked for me.

When I was in the middle of survival mode, I didn't take the time to notice what I was depending on, but afterward, I would marvel at how little I needed in my survival kit. This was contrary to everything I was reading in my baby apps, blogs, books, and anything else I could follow to prepare for my impending births. Turns out, pregnant ladies buy a lot of stuff (hello, nesting), so it's easy to sell things to them. But in reality, we don't need much. Women have been having babies since the beginning of time and have done just fine without all the "must-need" gadgets advertised in today's magazines. *Let's Choose Less* parenting starts during pregnancy. We begin with this mindset at the beginning, and hopefully it carries on through raising our children.

We start with the essentials and ask ourselves, "What is necessary for me to grow a healthy baby and have a safe, healthy delivery?" There are always "nice to haves," but the essentials are what we prioritize. Maternity clothes are necessary, but a closet full of maternity outfits is not. Hospital bags are great for added comfort during your stay in the hospital, but you don't actually need to pack a single thing. Everything you'd need for a stay at the hospital is already at the hospital! Postpartum supplies are necessary; there's not much wiggle room there. But the basics are easy to acquire and store. Each stage of pregnancy comes and goes so fast, so accumulating too much for each stage will quickly overwhelm you and your space before you even get to the part when there's a baby to care for.

Every pregnancy journey is different. The lists in this chapter contain my pregnancy and birth essentials with some nice-to-have options mixed in as well. There are inevitably items left off these lists, or by the time this book is published, something will be out of date, so use this as a tool for determining what your basics are and allow yourself to adapt as your situations evolve.

Maternity Wardrobe

Pregnancy is an important stage of your life. But soon it will pass, and the next season will start. (Although maybe tell that to a pregnant lady about thirty-seven weeks along when she's feeling like it will never end.) There are basic items that can get you through your pregnancy, but you can also protect your closet space, your bank account, and your mental health by avoiding excess.

Pregnancy can be overwhelming, and clutter will just add stress to the situation. Sticking to the essentials can help. As you progress through your pregnancy, ask yourself if you want or need it or before purchasing something. You need clothes to wear, but do you want to buy more than you need? Be purposeful about what you add so later you don't have the additional task of trying to decide what to take away.

Curate a capsule wardrobe as you purchase maternity clothes. Buy neutral or coordinating colors that can be interchanged and worn across multiple seasons. One nice coat or vest will be plenty to get you through winter, just like one cute maternity bathing suit will last you the summer. Pregnancy looks different for everyone. What I list here serves as the framework for what you may need. But if it's purposefully purchased, don't be afraid to think outside the mold and stick to what works best for you.

Spring/Summer Maternity Capsule Wardrobe Basics:

▶ **A cotton tank and denim shorts.** Probably not the first outfit you would think of, right? Having a solid pair of shorts you can throw on is a must-have for any warm-weather wardrobe, especially maternity. I often struggled with finding something to wear while pregnant because I didn't know what would fit or be comfortable. Having a standard pair of shorts— whether for a backyard party or just a random weekday outfit—helped immensely. I liked being able to know my dependable denim shorts would fit and look good no matter what part of pregnancy I was in. Pair with a solid color tank that can be layered or worn on its own.

▶ **A dependable, comfortable workout outfit.** If you're not a regular exerciser, this may not apply to you as much, but having a good workout outfit—or even just an awesome pair of leggings—can be the deciding factor for how active you are during your pregnancy.

With my earlier pregnancies, I didn't have many comfortable workout options, so I felt less inclined to exercise. When I discovered a good workout outfit option in my later pregnancies, I was able to feel comfortable working out up to my due dates. Having a good, comfy pair of leggings is very helpful, so I purchased several pairs of the same kind of pants so I wouldn't have to do laundry every day. Being active while you are pregnant, even just going for regular walks, is incredibly beneficial, but it's not possible if you don't have the right things to wear! I also enjoyed biking while I was pregnant. My all-time favorite pregnancy bike shorts were Lululemon Aligns in a size or two up from my normal size.

▶ **A comfortable, cute dress (or two).** Having a comfortable dress that will look nice and not require too much thought or time getting ready is essential to any mom's wardrobe, but it's paramount for a maternity wardrobe. As someone who has struggled with body image in the past, I tried not to spend too much time worrying about clothes while pregnant, but this becomes increasingly difficult when you are outgrowing your clothes all the time. I found that having an easy, comfortable, nice-looking dress can make a huge difference. Two or three will make your whole summer easier. Just rotate which one you pick and know that you will feel comfortable and look good!

▶ **A maternity bathing suit.** I put myself through some uncomfortable maternity bathing suit experiences on beach trips over the years, and it made me not want to take those trips. One year for my birthday, my mom gifted me with a spectacular maternity bathing suit, and it made a monumental difference for our summer. One bathing suit is all it takes!

▶ **A nice pair of nursing/maternity pajamas.** Right after our oldest was born, my mom showed up at the hospital with a present for me. I thought it was one of the kindest things someone could do for a new mom, so I've tried to do the same for friends. Instead of buying the baby presents, it's so nice to have a practical gift for the new mom. The gift my mom gave me was a nice maternity/nursing pajama dress. At first, I didn't think I would use it much, but I was incredibly grateful for her gesture. Moms indeed know best, because I quickly realized my postpartum body wouldn't fit into most of my old pajamas—plus none were nursing-friendly. I ended up purchasing several more just like the ones she gave me, and they have served me well through all my pregnancies and years of nursing. Not only did they fit throughout my entire pregnancy, but the added ease during nursing sessions was invaluable. I found them to feel so much better than an oversized T-shirt when I was already feeling frumpy, especially in the first few weeks postpartum.

I would say this is an all-year maternity wardrobe that's "nice to have" but not necessary. You can always opt for a comfy T-shirt from your spouse's drawer instead!

Fall/Winter Maternity Capsule Wardrobe Basics:

▶ **Maternity jeans.** A dependable, good-fitting pair of maternity jeans can be worn throughout the fall and winter. You only need one pair, or maybe two, to make it through. Invest in one nice pair versus filling your closet with several "OK" options.

▶ **A jacket or vest.** I was always very warm during pregnancy and never purchased a maternity coat, but I did have a fabulous puffy vest that worked perfectly for really cold days. An added benefit was that it didn't take up much room to store between pregnancies and seasons.

▶ **Maternity leggings.** Want to know a secret? My favorite maternity leggings were not maternity at all. I used the same few pairs of Lululemon Align extra-high-rise leggings in a size or two up from my normal size for multiple pregnancies and postpartum journeys. (Also, if you don't tell anyone, I'll tell you that years later, they are still my favorite leggings.) Invest in a good quality pair, and you won't regret it.

Two to four pairs will be more than enough, but if you do laundry frequently, you could have even fewer pairs.

▶ **Layering tanks.** My temperature would fluctuate vastly during pregnancy, so having a tank as a bottom layer always guaranteed that I could cool off when I needed to, even in the winter. Two to three should be just the right number.

▶ **A cardigan/sweater or two.** You don't need many, but a few sweaters will go a long way for your growing belly. Here's where your capsule wardrobe skills can come into play. Find a sweater you love and purchase it in a few colors that will match all the maternity bottoms you have. This will keep the decision-making process easy when getting dressed.

▶ **Supportive bras.** The less pretty the bra, the more supportive it likely is. Pregnancy is not the time to look for pretty bras. You need the ones that will keep everything feeling supported, and this can help prevent back pain. Bonus points if your maternity bras are also nursing bras so you don't have to repurchase all your bras when the baby is born.

▶ **Maternity underwear.** Regardless of the season, you may want to add a few new pairs of underwear to your drawer. Some ladies never need these, and others swear by them. Remember that pregnancy is a personal journey, and there's no wrong way. Comfort is most important when it comes to most things, especially underwear.

Maternity Capsule Wardrobe Examples:

Spring/Summer:

- 2-3 warm weather dresses
- 2-3 flowy short-sleeve shirts
- 1 maternity bathing suit
- 2-3 nursing/maternity tank tops
- 1-2 pairs of maternity shorts
- 1-2 pairs of pajamas (optional)
- 2 nursing/maternity bras
- 1 dependable (good quality) workout outfit

Fall/Winter:

- 2-3 cold weather dresses
- 2-3 flowy long-sleeve shirts
- 2-3 nursing/maternity tank tops
- 1 pair of maternity jeans
- 1 pair of (good quality) leggings
- 1-2 sweaters
- 1-2 pairs of pajamas (optional)
- 2 nursing/maternity bras
- 1 dependable (good quality) workout outfit
- 1 jacket or vest

Wardrobe Exceptions:

I'm not in your closet or your climate, so I won't tell you to "never" purchase something. If your job requires you to wear certain types of clothes, you may need to add more of something to your wardrobe. I was a dance teacher while pregnant, so I had a large collection of leggings and oversize T-shirts, but not much in the way of formal wear. If you work in a corporate environment, however, you might need some nice slacks or "business casual" dresses. You may live in an area that requires more of a certain type of clothing. The key is to remember that you will likely have to switch your clothes fairly frequently since your size will change throughout your pregnancy, and whatever items you add to your wardrobe, you will have to store them once you're finished using them. I loved being able to leave some non-maternity items in my wardrobe rotations like my favorite cardigans, cozy oversized sweatpants, flowy and very stretchy shirts from non-pregnant times, or even just a comfy T-shirt I grabbed from Jon's drawer. Not all items you wear when you're pregnant need to be purchased new.

Non-Clothing Maternity Essentials:

▶ **Prenatal vitamins.** No exceptions on this one: Just take your vitamins. Find the ones you can stomach and order them in bulk. You'll need them when you are postpartum as well.

▶ **Maternity pillow.** Truly not a must-have, but this is a very nice-to-have item. Sleep is hard enough when you're pregnant, so a maternity pillow might keep you a little more comfortable.

▶ **Body/belly butter.** Any part of you that grows during pregnancy needs some body butter. Apply after your shower for extra absorption and keep applying once you have your baby and your body continues to change.

▶ **Mattress protector.** This will be very helpful for post-partum, but it's also great to have during pregnancy in case your water breaks while you're in bed.

Maternity Items You Can Do Without:

▶ **Gimmicky subscriptions.** Plenty of apps and sub-scription services will send you free products or notifications for every small kick. It's a fast way to get your information to a lot of people who want to sell you products.

▶ **Waistband extenders.** If you feel the need to purchase these, it might be time to look into maternity pants. They will be more comfortable!

All of this is contingent on what works for you. If you love high heels and want to wear them throughout your pregnancy, more power to you. That just wasn't for me. Being a pregnant essentialist means taking a hard look at your wardrobe and recognizing that you don't need to buy all the influencer outfits. Comfort is paramount during pregnancy, so if it fits and feels good, I say go for it.

Hospital Essentials

How early is too early to pack your hospital bag? If you're me, it was at about twenty weeks. But as you may have guessed by now, I was a little overzealous in my preparations. If it helps you sleep at night, prepare your bag whenever you'd like! Just promise me you won't pack enough to seem like you're moving into the hospital.

Before you put a single item in your bag, remember that the hospital has everything you might need during your stay, so all that you bring with you is for your own comfort. Many women arrive at the hospital without a hospital bag, and they do just fine.

Now head to the closet and grab a medium-sized tote bag, preferably something that has a wipeable surface—and bonus if it has pockets. A few packing cubes or some Ziploc bags will come in handy to keep things organized.

Of all the things I've learned from my previous birth experiences, one major thing I seemed to always forget was how much extra stuff the hospital sends home with you. Whether it was spare nursing supplies, baby diapers, postpartum supplies, pamphlets and booklets, paperwork, or sentimental items, I was amazed at how much we would collect.

So as you pack, leave plenty of room for extras or include an extra bag in your hospital bag for overflow.

Let's start packing!

Miscellaneous Items:

I always tried to pack a lot of items that could be left behind. I would start to collect toiletries that were almost finished or hotel toiletries throughout my pregnancy, old socks, spare donation clothes, and anything else that I would be fine getting messy or leaving behind. As with anything in today's world, there is always a mindful way to dispose of items, but childbirth is messy, so I'll leave it up to you how you feel about disposable versus washable items.

▶ **Postpartum supplies.** Not a must, but I loved using my things more than what the hospital provides. I used mainly Frida Mom products; the maxi-pad ice packs are lifesavers. If you want to bring less, you can eliminate all of this as the hospital has everything you'll need.

▶ **Nursing pads.** For a one- to two-day stay, pack six to eight nursing pads, depending on whom you ask. Many women say it isn't necessary, but they were wonderful for me.

▶ **Phone charger.** Pack this ahead of time so you don't have to worry about grabbing one on the way out the door. Bonus points if you pack one that is extralong because the hospital outlets are always far from the beds.

▶ **Snacks.** Postdelivery hunger is unrivaled, and if the kitchen is closed, you may have to wait a while for food. Keep some protein bars or small snacks on hand.

▶ **Old flip-flops.** You'll use these to walk to the bathroom and use in the shower.

▶ **Specialty baby items**. A nameplate, a special blanket with the baby's name on it, hairbows, or hats—a few items go a long way in this category!

▶ **Baby book supplies inside an empty binder.** Include a pen and extra paper for notes. I love having Jon jot down labor notes and things we remember from the delivery as soon as he can to save some of those very special memories that may not be remembered as clearly later. It's also super helpful for reminders like calling your pediatrician and storing all your new pamphlets and paperwork until you can sort through it all.

▶ **Garbage bag.** You'll be glad you have this for dirty laundry.

▶ **Pillow.** This is a "nice-to-have" but not a "have-to-have" item. If you're going for minimalist packing, you may not want to bring one, but if you're looking for some comfort from home, then feel free to pack it! Just remember to bring a nonwhite pillowcase so your pillow from home doesn't get lost in the stack of hospital pillows.

▶ **Sound machine.** Another nice-to-have, but not a must. Some ladies like to drown out the noise of the hallway, but this can also do such a good job of drowning out noise that you don't hear nurses coming in and out of your room.

Toiletries:

Try to save products that are almost running out, and then you can recycle or throw away empty bottles and not have to unpack them later. Pack in a Ziplock bag or a clear toiletry bag to make it easier to find things:

▶ Face lotion

▶ Face wash

▶ Lip balm

▶ Hand lotion

▶ Toothbrush

▶ Toothpaste

▶ Dental floss

▶ Shower supplies

▶ Deodorant

Clothing:

▸ **Two pairs of comfortable, loose-fitting pajamas.** Save your nice clothes for going home when you'll actually see people. Many women wear the hospital gowns their entire stay, but I appreciated having my own clothes to wear as well.

▸ **A robe.** You never know what the temperature will be like in your room, so it's helpful to have an extra layer just in case.

▸ **Socks.** The hospital will provide some for you, so these aren't an absolute necessity, but if there's room in your bag, you might appreciate a comfy pair of socks from home.

▸ **Going home outfit for Mom.** What you will want to wear home is totally up to you. I usually pick a maternity dress because I know it will fit and feel comfortable.

▸ **Two to three baby outfits/gown and baby blankets.** Not necessary, but it's so nice to have clean clothes that smell like home to wrap your baby in. You can eliminate a lot of extra stuff if you don't bring any of these, but an outfit or two always feels nice.

Items for Dad:

This section is flexible. Jon usually didn't bring much and would head home at some point to change clothes, shower, let the dog out, etc., so he packed the bare minimum. Depending on how long you are going to be staying, your spouse may need more things. The hospital typically provides the patient with everything they need, but not the partner. (The same goes for food.) When we stayed at the hospital, meals always were only for me and not supposed to be for Jon. I would typically order something we could split, or he would pick something up from the cafeteria. The linens provided weren't the highest quality, but if you plan on getting a lot of sleep in the hospital, you might want to reframe your mindset. Spouses typically need the following:

- Change of clothes (prioritize clothing that would be easy for skin to skin)
- Toiletries for Dad (don't forget contact solution!)
- iPad, phone, charger
- Snacks/water
- Extra layers or a spare blanket

Items You Don't Need for the Hospital:

- **Your own delivery gown.** I brought my own for one of my deliveries, and by the time I was able to get home and stain-treat it, it was ruined. Just let the hospital handle this one.

▶ **Core support belt.** Too soon! Wait until you are home for a while before attempting to use this unless your providers suggest you use one. If that's the case, the hospital will have one for you to use.

▶ **Breastfeeding pillow.** If you choose to use one, you likely won't be able to fit into it while you're in the hospital. Save this for when you get home and bring it to your lactation consultant appointments instead.

▶ **Breast pump.** If you need one, the hospital will have one you can use along with all the parts.

▶ **Nursing cover.** Especially if you're a first-time mom, you might think you need to pack one for the hospital. But you will likely not have enough hands to use it in addition to trying to figure out how to breastfeed.

Items to Bring That Won't Necessarily Fit into Your Dedicated Hospital Bag:

▶ **The baby's car seat.** Have your partner bring it into the hospital just before you leave so you don't have to carry it from labor to recovery. Pro tip: install the car seat base before you go into labor so you aren't exhausted trying to figure out how to install it as you leave the hospital.

▶ **Your purse, your phone, your insurance card, and your ID.** (You will need to grab these when it's "go-time" instead of having them on standby in your hospital bag.)

You and your partner can have your packed bags next to each other's so he can grab both on the way out the door when you leave for the hospital.

Postpartum Essentials

Getting ready for a new baby takes a ton of work. Chances are if you're expecting or know someone who is, she's probably focusing her "preparation energy" mostly on things the baby will need and may have forgotten what *she* might need as a new mom. (Guilty as charged, on multiple occasions.)

As a mom of four, I had my postpartum supply list and timing down to a science by baby number four. Around the same time you're getting your hospital bag packed, get your postpartum supplies in order.

▶ **Postpartum supplies.** The hospital provides you with these items, but it made a big difference for me when I brought my own supplies to the hospital. Frida Mom was my favorite to pack for recovery in the hospital and at home. The maxi-pad ice packs are amazing. Once I was home, I used Always Depends until I didn't need them anymore. Maxi pads were uncomfortable to sit on while I was trying to recover.

Just embrace the stage and remember that you'll be out of it soon!

▶ **Adult diapers.** These are way better than maxi pads. You can also add witch hazel and aloe to some and then freeze for a "pad-cicle" to help with recovery.

▶ **Stool softener.** Nothing is scarier than those first few postpartum BMs.

▶ **Perineal spray.** Dermoplast is usually at the hospital, so you can grab that to bring home—and it works great.

▶ **Nursing pads.** I typically went with disposable ones, but there are wonderful washable ones as well.

▶ **Gel soothing nipple pads.** These will make a big difference in the early days.

▶ **Lanolin cream.** Trust me on this one.

▶ **Peri bottle.** There will be one at the hospital for you, but I would bring my own (Frida Mom) that was a little easier to use.

▶ **Haakaa.** This didn't exist when I had my first baby, but once I got one, it was a game changer. Get the one with the cap because it's heartbreaking to knock over in the middle of the night. I used this instead of a pump plenty of times and was so glad I had it.

▶ **Nursing pillow.** Not a must-have and many lactation consultants recommend not getting one. If you do choose to get one, it's absolutely a personal choice which one you use. I went with "My Breast Friend" for all my kids.

▶ **Loose, forgiving clothes.** It doesn't matter what brand or if they are new—just that you can wear them comfortably and they give you easy nursing access. I love nursing pajama dresses for the immediate postpartum time and then usually opt for a loose shirt and leggings as time goes on.

▶ **Nursing bra.** After nursing four different kids for almost a year each, I think I can safely say I know what I want out of a nursing bra, and the least cute ones were always the most comfortable.

▶ **A heavy-duty water bottle.** Fill up a massive bottle to have next to your bed or nursing station overnight. I typically used my Hydro Flask or Stanley cup overnight and then something a little less bulky during the day.

▶ **Nursing entertainment.** It doesn't matter what you choose, but have a plan for something to entertain you. Staying awake during the overnight feedings can be hard, and having something to entertain you helps. Whether it's the library app, a good podcast, a new vlog episode, or a binge-worthy TV series, find something that can keep you awake.

▶ **Frozen foods.** If someone asks you for a baby gift idea, instead of asking for an actual gift, ask for a frozen meal. Or do what I do and just stock your freezer with Trader Joe's and Costco frozen meal options.

▶ **Pumping supplies.** Even if you don't plan to pump or bottle feed, it is always better to be prepared.

▶ **A comfortable nursing nook.** Make yourself a little nursing or pumping corner in each section of your house. For me, upstairs in my bedroom is always the first spot and downstairs I have a comfy recliner with a table next to it.

▶ **Waterproof mattress protector for your bed.** Night sweats, leaking, and any other bodily fluids your baby might add to the mix will end up in your bed. Protect your mattress.

Postpartum Items You Don't Need:

▶ **A full calendar.** Clear your schedules, stay home, and give yourself plenty of time to recover.

▶ **A sitz bath.** If you have a bathtub that will work just as well; you don't need to take up the space of a dedicated sitz bath.

While I would say there are plenty of other things you could add to any of these lists, with modern-day online shopping, you can get what you need as you need it, so it's better not to get too much in advance. Online overnight Amazon shopping is fair game when you are feeding a newborn, and there will always be something you need but didn't think of in advance. Just have the essentials for the first few days and then order or have someone pick up what you need. You can't anticipate absolutely everything you may need before the baby comes. Every baby is different, and you might end up needing something you never expected . . . like more bibs and burp cloths!

You can read all the books and Google everything you can think of about delivering a baby, but there's always something you'll wish you had been told beforehand. The nitty gritty. The truly honest. The things that only the closest people you know can tell you without offending you or really scaring you. If there's one thing that I would tell someone getting ready to have a baby—regardless of what number child this is for them—it would be to *find someone that understands and let them help you.* Tell that person how you really feel and don't be afraid to be vulnerable. Having just one person who can help you feel heard or validated can make all the difference in your pregnancy and postpartum journey. Someone you can show your true feelings to, knowing you are loved and cared for while trying to find your way through pregnancy and postpartum life, is more important than any other "new parenting tip."

Pregnancy is a wild ride. You change sizes faster than you can get your shoes on, your body likes something one day and hates it the next, and you are constantly relearning yourself while trying to figure out how to bring a kid from inside of you to outside. It can be overwhelming, exhausting, really hot (pregnancy in the summer . . . OMG), and did I mention exhausting? All around it's a roller coaster that feels never-ending, and then it ends way too quickly. The best-laid plans are the ones that never go accordingly. No matter how impeccably detailed your supply list is, there will be something you forgot. Even if you have the world's most strategically packed hospital bag (ahem—looking at myself), you will still think of something you didn't need to bring or wish you had.

Every delivery experience is different, so you will never be 100 percent prepared. *Let's Choose Less* is not foolproof, nor will it guarantee the ideal pregnancy or delivery, but it will help you maintain focus on what's truly important: delivering a healthy baby as safely as possible. Which is far more important than if you made sure to pack lip balm in your hospital bag. Keep your eyes on the journey, not on the materials, so you don't miss a single part of the experience. And give yourself some grace along the way.

This chapter focuses on the physical items that will help you in the pregnancy and postpartum stages. It is not intended to address mental health issues of any kind. It is a beautiful thing to ask for help. Always seek professional guidance if you are feeling anxious, depressed, or any other condition.

LET'S CHOOSE LESS PREGNANCY AND BIRTH DOS:

- ▶ Do ask yourself if something is a want or a need when purchasing maternity supplies.
- ▶ Do pack a hospital bag when you're ready and have your partner do the same.
- ▶ Do curate a maternity capsule wardrobe.
- ▶ Do stock up on postpartum supplies.

LET'S CHOOSE LESS PREGNANCY AND BIRTH DON'TS:

- ▶ Don't buy everything the lists tell you to.
- ▶ Don't fill your closet with maternity clothes.
- ▶ Don't forget that this is all a season that will pass.

Journal Prompt/Discussion Questions:

▶ Where are you planning to store your maternity items?

▶ Do you have something that will be an essential for you during pregnancy?

▶ What are you most looking forward to about a pregnancy journey?

CHAPTER 9

THE FIRST YEAR—
HOW MUCH DOES A
BABY REALLY NEED?

You are the most important
thing in your child's life.

B abies are my favorite. Don't get me wrong, kids are awesome, too, but there's something so uniquely special about a sweet, brand-new, squishy baby. They require so little yet SO much. Life with a newborn is exhausting and blurry, but it also can be really simple. Their needs boil down to hunger, tiredness, and discomfort. The schedule is basic: eat and sleep when you can. The goal is straightforward: keep the tiny human safe and fed.

Their growth is so tangible and swift that you swear they look bigger today than yesterday because they definitely are. Everything is tiny and adorable. Itty-bitty diapers, teeny-tiny onesies, and precious little toes. In a blink, they are no longer curled-up newborns but drooling, babbling, moving balls of activity. They learn to smile, sit up, eat real food, walk, and identify their favorite people, and before you know it, the endless, sleepless newborn nights are far beyond you. Babies don't keep, and that's part of what makes them my favorite.

The season of having a baby is short, yet it feels never-ending when you're in the middle of it. Nothing seems harder than trying to change a diaper on a squirmy newborn at 3:00 a.m. with only an hour of sleep, but somehow you make it through. This is what I didn't hear before I had kids. You *do* make it to the other side.

In all the books I read as an expectant mother, not a single book told me what *not* to buy for my baby, just all the things I *should* buy. I never read that seasons change quickly. That having a baby is a beautiful yet challenging time that will someday come to an end. What I did hear and read plenty of was "must have" lists, sample registry options, and important gear you "MUST BUY." Plenty of tips on how to prepare for your baby were easy to find but very little beyond the mythical "fourth trimester" that everyone focuses on. Most importantly, no one ever told me it was okay to not listen to all the noise I was hearing.

If you take nothing else from the pages of this chapter, hear this: Your baby needs very little stuff when he or she is born. *You are the most important thing in your child's life.* You. Just you. Whether it's your first baby or your twelfth, it's all the same. All that sweet little new life needs is you.

From the moment you share your pregnancy news outside of your relationship with your partner, you will be given advice and information from everyone. Your sister will have a great app for you to track your pregnancy, your best friend will send over her favorite maternity books, and your mom will want you to start a registry online so she can plan your baby shower. Each app, website, great-aunt, and well-meaning stranger at the grocery store checkout will offer you unsolicited advice while quizzing you on which items you've purchased already. "Are you ready for baby to arrive?" and "What else do you need for the nursery?" will become the most-asked questions you'll hear, only surpassed by "How are you feeling?" Bringing a child into the world is intimidating enough, so don't be afraid to block out the pressure from others no matter how well meaning they are. Sign up for the websites or apps you're interested in, but if you feel like it isn't adding value to your preparations, just unsubscribe.

Resist the urge to buy all the supplies you think you need before your baby arrives. Allow yourself to determine what you think is necessary for your home and your baby. If you don't want a bassinet, don't get one! You are allowed to register for only things you want or not register for anything at all. This is where all the hard work of implementing *Let's Choose Less* starts to pay off. You can say no if something doesn't align with your family values.

The items in your home reflect your values, especially when you have a baby. Every family is different; therefore what my family needs is not necessarily what yours will need. Take all the information presented to you in this stage of life and use the parts that seem most essential to you. I'm not saying you shouldn't register for absolutely anything (although no judgment here if that's your choice), but I am saying you have the power to determine what items are most necessary for your child.

In the following pages, I share what I found to be the most essential items for my kids from birth through age one. What worked for us will likely not be a perfect match for you, but I'm here to be a guide. Learn from my experience but also from your own. Information is a tool to help you make the best decision you can with the current knowledge you have. I'll never forget how important I thought a baby wipe warmer was for our registry with Emily and how much I didn't use it. Don't let the perfect choice of stroller be the enemy of a good choice based on what you know at the time. Trust me, you'll likely end up selling the one you register for and getting a different one anyway. Turn down the noise of the world and listen to what you think is best. This is your family and your baby!

The Essential Nursery

Let's get this part out of the way first. *You do not need to have a beautiful nursery to have a baby.* There are no prerequisites for bringing a baby home that lists a completed nursery. It's simply not necessary. For four beautiful children, we never had a perfectly prepared nursery, and our kids are more than fine. Your baby will likely not even use their room for weeks if not months after being born, so I think we are all in agreement that the perfect gender-neutral wall color won't matter during diaper changes in the middle of the night. If getting the nursery in order is at the top of your nesting/baby preparation list or it brings you great joy and excitement to have finished, don't let me stand in your way! A beautifully curated space for your baby might be just the thing to help you feel prepared to bring your baby home, but if it doesn't happen that's OK too.

Now that we've established that the state of the nursery is not vital to the birthing checklist, there are a few items you will actually benefit from having on hand when you bring your little bundle of joy home.

What You *Actually* Need for a New Baby:

- ▶ **A place for baby to sleep.** We usually started with a bassinet in our room and then once our babies were ready, we transitioned to a pack-n-play in our room or to a crib in their room. Some babies do not like a bassinet. (Emily, our oldest, was not a fan at all. But Maggie, our third, loved hers.) Bassinets are not vital. They can be huge and a pain to store or move, so if you have space that's great, but you can also go right to the pack-n-play or crib. The choice of where you think the baby should sleep is yours; just make sure it's safe.

▶ **A secondary safe place for baby to lie down.** This is especially important if you have older kids or even a dog. We kept a pack-n-play in our living room for the first several months for diaper changes and as a contained space where baby could rest or play without being on the floor or in a low chair at risk of being bumped or stepped on by an older sibling. I'll never forget sweet Emily trying to be helpful by pushing Sophie in her newborn swing. A place where a big-hearted older sibling can see but not touch is a really good idea.

▶ **Car seat.** This is a nonnegotiable. Gotta have one unless you live in a big city where you won't need one!

▶ **Diapers and wipes.** We were big fans of Honest diapers and wipes in our house, but you'll figure out which brand you and your baby prefer. Have a small selection of newborn size diapers and some larger size ones on hand as well. We brought at least two babies home from the hospital in size one diapers. Cloth diapers are a cool concept if that is something for you. Leave yourself open to the idea that your baby's skin may not approve of your choice and give yourself some grace as you adjust accordingly.

▶ **Diaper cream.** We've tried so many different kinds but have always gravitated back to Aquaphor. It's what has worked best for us, but just like diapers, you'll find what works for you and your baby!

▶ **Clothes.** Obviously your little one needs something to wear, but they really don't need as much as you think. I find that everyone loves to gift baby clothes, and we always ended up with way more outfits in small sizes than we needed. If you are creating a registry, add larger sizes for later or even clothing store gift cards instead of registering for all newborn or three-month size clothes. If you plan to do laundry every day, you can get by with even less, but I would say you don't need more than twelve to fifteen outfits at most. Remember, baby clothes are small, so it's easy to accumulate a lot because they don't take up a ton of space! There's a sample capsule wardrobe later in this chapter for baby's first year of life. There are more than enough outfits listed, especially when you consider different sizes. For me, newborn gowns outweigh all other outfits for at least the first three months. They have snaps to adjust from gown to sleeper, make diaper changes a breeze, and work great with the umbilical cord in the early days. If you want to register for minimal clothing, newborn gowns are at the top of the list. Any seasoned mom will say that zipper or magnetic onesies are the way to go!

▶ **Baby blankets.** Here's why it isn't as important to have too many clothes. You'll probably keep the baby wrapped up most of the time, which will cover up all their outfits. Blankets are also great for burp cloths if you don't want to have too many things to juggle. It is helpful to have a few different kinds of blankets for different purposes. Some are bigger and work great for swaddling, while others are better for covering car seats or laying down for playing on the floor.

▶ **Baby wrap or carrier.** Babywearing is everything, especially if you have other kids. A good baby wrap will free your hands to help your older kids, feed yourself, give you a chance to go to the bathroom, and can replace multiple bouncy seats. It can save your posture from holding baby all the time, and I bet it's also where your baby will nap most of the time. Babies only want to be close to Mom, and a good baby wrap can keep everyone happy.

▶ **Pump and bottle supplies.** Babies can be picky with their bottles, so I wouldn't stock up too much on one kind of bottle until you know for sure they will work. You can apply to get a breast pump through your insurance provider or choose a specific one to purchase by yourself. A Haakaa is an excellent alternative to catch let-down milk on your opposite side when nursing or for a quick pump option.

▶ **Baby first aid.** I was taken completely off guard the first time we needed baby Tylenol and realized we didn't have the right kind. Do your research ahead of time so when baby has his or her first fever, you aren't making a midnight pharmacy run for the right kind of meds like we did.

▶ **Stroller.** This is a big-ticket item that you don't absolutely need right off the bat. It's nice to have for neighborhood walks or adventures to the mall, but it's not necessary when you can also baby wear. Strollers can be expensive, so this is a great item to have on your registry, and others can help with the purchasing if you have a place to store the stroller until you're ready to use. This is also a great item to get on consignment or from a neighborhood Facebook group later on.

▶ **Burp cloths.** OK, stay with me for a minute. I used burp cloths, and they were great, but they aren't an *absolute* necessity. As I mentioned, you can always multipurpose your baby blankets if need be. I did both. In a bind, if you're out somewhere or if space is an issue at home, burp cloths are nice to have but not a must-have. We loved using cloth diapers as burp cloths. They are extra absorbent and held up wonderfully through all four of our kids.

▶ **High chair.** There are many different kinds of high chairs. You'll have to decide which one is best for your space and family. We had one that was easily wiped down, and it was the best for our messy eaters.

Capsule Wardrobe for Baby's First Year:

Warm Weather	Cold Weather
6 to 12 onesies	6 to 12 onesies
5 short-sleeve shirts (or dresses)	5 long-sleeve shirts
3 to 5 pairs of shorts	3 to 5 pairs of pants
5 to 7 pairs of jammies	5 to 7 pairs of jammies
2 sweaters	3 to 5 sweaters
2 swimsuits	1 or 2 coats

Things You Don't Need for a Baby:

▶ **Toys.** We are talking babies here; they don't need a bunch of toys. Maybe one or two in the diaper bag to hang on the car seat and a few at home (like a pack-n-play with toys), but don't go overboard with toys for your newborn. Even as they get older, kids don't need a lot of toys. It's a great way to lay the *Let's Choose Less* foundation and start this habit early.

▶ **A full closet of outfits.** Babies grow fast. Don't waste your space and money on too many newborn or zero to three-month outfits. Spread the love over all the sizes. You'll be amazed at how fast babies grow out of some of those cute little onesies and then you have to figure out what to do with all the clothes they never wore.

▶ **Shoes.** Another "nice to have" but really not a "need to have" until your baby is truly walking. Once they are walking, invest in good quality shoes that will aid in healthy development. I'm sorry to say that the cute shoes aren't always the best ones for little feet. If you live in a colder climate, a good pair of fleece booties is a great investment to keep those little toes warm!

▶ **Single-purpose bulky items.** Bassinets, swings, bouncy seats, exersaucers, and jumpers are all awesome, but you have no idea what your baby will like until he or she is at that stage. We had an awesome exersaucer that Emily hated and never used. We saved it for Sophie, and she loved it. These items are all great if they work but a huge pain to store for later if they don't. Your best option is to borrow before you buy or try selling if you need to replace it with something similar. Babies use items in this category for a short amount of time, and then for the rest of the time you own that item, you'll have to figure out where or how to store it. This is a great category for getting creative by borrowing or renting.

As a general rule, it is better to have less starting off because you have no idea what your baby will actually like and you may end up having to purchase something completely different than what you already have. Babies also grow out of everything way faster than you'd think. Bouncy seats and swings are great, but you can only use them for a short time before they become lovely living room decorations. Baby clothes are made like Shrinky Dinks (remember those?) to be half the size once you wash them. So don't stock up on too many small sizes; you'll need bigger ones way sooner than you think. The good news is that the internet is always open so you can order whatever you need once the baby has arrived if you find that you don't have it already. I would also suggest looking into local mom buy, sell, and trade groups on Facebook for used items that you can resell once you're finished with them instead of storing them. The secondhand baby and kid gear industry is booming, so if you aren't finding much luck in online groups, I'm sure you'll be able to find a church sale or children's consignment shop nearby.

At the back of the book, you'll find a sample baby registry list to help make your baby shopping and preparations a little less complicated. I'm careful to not list too many brands because there are so many good ones to choose from, but also brands are a personal choice. Car seats alone have more brands than the spice section in the grocery store! If you're having trouble deciding between brands on a particular item, I suggest writing out what is most important to you when it comes to this item and seeing if it helps eliminate some options. I always opt for the safest option that is reasonably priced. The next best option for figuring out what brand to buy is to try something out. You test drive a car before you purchase, so why not baby gear? Ask a friend or a neighbor if you can push their stroller around for a few minutes to see how it feels or install one of their car seats in your car to know if it will fit. Moms love to talk about baby gear, so don't be afraid to make a new friend at the mall or the consignment store when trying to decide.

Baby Diaper Bag

New parents can always be spotted a mile away based on the size of their diaper bags. The more kids a family has, the smaller their diaper bag. As we progress through the book, you'll find diaper bag packing lists for each of the younger ages, and we cover what to have on hand as the kids get older. (Hint: We rely more on our car to keep supplies for "just in case" scenarios.)

Now that our kids are older, I use a sling backpack. If it's an option, always pick the backpack style of diaper bag, since you'll need your hands free. When picking a diaper bag, look for ones that can be wiped clean inside and out, are made with really durable materials that won't show a lot of wear, and can hold a lot but aren't overly bulky. Fashion does not always equal practicality, especially when it comes to diaper bags.

It's just as important to choose the right diaper bag as it is to choose the right things that go into the bag. The easy answer for diaper bag essentials is that it's different every time you leave the house, and it's a personal choice for what you think is most important to carry. Keeping a standard set of supplies like wipes, hand sanitizer, and a changing pad helps minimize packing fatigue. Packing for where you are going is easier than trying to anticipate everything you might need for every excursion out of the house. If we need water bottles, I pack them. If we are going out to eat, I grab extra wipes or a disposable placemat. On a good day, I don't have enough hands to carry everyone and everything, so my diaper bag is also my purse. I keep items like keys, phone, wallet, gum, lip balm, hand sanitizer, lotion, a few first aid items, and a pen in a smaller bag or pouch within the diaper bag.

The younger your kids are, the larger your diaper bag will be. In our big diaper bag days, we typically had two sets of supplies: one in the main portion of my backpack that included wipes, diapers (usually six to eight on hand and more in the car), and disposable changing pads, plus a small removable diaper clutch I could grab out of my bag for fast diaper changes. This small clutch was especially handy for small spaces where I could grab everything I needed without having to sift through the rest of the bag. Disposable changing pads were a game changer. They are thin and easy to pack but contain all the mess. Spare outfits are always necessary on the go, but within your diaper bag, two outfit changes should be more than enough. If you need more, you can keep some in your car. Plastic bags are useful for messy diapers, dirty clothes, and all the laundry you'll likely accumulate. I like using a "wet-dry bag" for messy laundry on the go and then throw it all—bag included—in the washing machine when I get home. A few teethers or a small book is plenty in the toy category for any baby under the age of one.

Obviously, in the first year there will be bottles and milk to bring along before snacks are on the table. This will be different for each child and family! Snacks will need to be repacked each time you leave the house, depending on your baby's developmental stage. Anything you pack will have to be carried along with whatever else you accumulate during your outing, so the more spare room in your diaper bag, the better because it will likely fill up! The more kids you have, the easier it is to rationalize carrying less so you are still able to keep up with everyone and be prepared for whatever you might need while away from home.

Diaper Bag Essentials for Baby:

- ▶ Mom's purse supplies
- ▶ 6 to 8 diapers and a pack of wipes
- ▶ Changing pad
- ▶ 2 or 3 spare outfits
- ▶ Hand sanitizer or cleaning wipes
- ▶ 2 or 3 toys
- ▶ Plastic trash bags and a wet-dry bag
- ▶ First aid supplies

Age One

Ah, the one-year-old. A friend of mine once told me that when you have a baby, you forget they won't always be that little. Then one day they start talking and walking, and even though you knew it was going to happen, it still takes you by complete surprise. It's as though your cat suddenly decided to start having a conversation with you. By the time your baby turns one, he or she will still be themselves personality-wise, but almost everything else will have drastically changed since their birth. The sleepless newborn nights don't seem as scary as they did a few months ago, especially compared to watching your toddler learn to walk on concrete.

The seasons shift, and so do the necessities. One-year-olds need different things than babies, and now all your hard work from baby preparation has paid off.

One-year-olds have a huge span of developmental stages, which is why it helps to keep only the basics in your home. Growth in the first two years of life is immensely rapid. By the time a child gets to their second birthday, developmental stages slow down a little, and change doesn't happen as quickly. This means that from the first to the second birthday, in the span of a single year, almost all your "kid equipment" will be used and then become unnecessary. A twelve-month-old has very different needs than a twenty-three-month-old when it comes to essential items and toys. Choosing specialized items can be great for a particular stage, but it's also where a lot of clutter in your home can come from. If you have a fourteen-month-old who is really into tractors, follow that line of interest within reason. Don't buy every tractor you can find—next week it might be trains instead, and you'll have a house full of unused tractors.

Try to borrow or rent anything before buying at this stage, as your child will likely outgrow it quickly, and then you'll have to figure out where to store it. Our local area is teeming with Facebook groups for moms to sell and purchase used kids' clothes or gear. It has allowed us to have some entertaining or helpful items without needing to store them once we're finished with them. It's a huge advantage to have a friend or family member with whom to share equipment. If your neighbor has a child a little older than yours, you may be able to borrow their bassinet while they borrow your wagon. Sometimes I joke that I store our stuff at other people's houses, which is actually a really savvy way to make use of things while not having to repurchase or store them.

As your child learns how to do something, they will want to repeat it relentlessly until they master that skill. Repetition is everything to a one-year-old. Whether it's walking, running, figuring out how to stack items, using utensils, climbing stairs, saying "no," drinking out of a cup, or pulling hair, each skill will be practiced repeatedly. One of the best things you can do for your kids at this age is to have your home set up for safe exploration and mastery of skills. Put up those baby gates if you haven't already, buy some squishy mats for indoor play, and gather kid-sized versions of common household tools for little helpers. Wherever you are and whatever you're doing, your child will likely want to be involved at this age. A small broom or mop can turn chores into a learning activity. This can be where you begin cultivating independence in your child. Allow your little one to attempt to carry their own plate, perform personal hygiene, help prepare food, tidy around the house, get dressed, put on their own shoes, put laundry away, and more. What we think of as work is play to our kids at this age. Giving your child these opportunities will never result in a clean home or a quick execution, but it will foster their sense of wonder and further their pursuit to learn from all aspects of life around them.

The most influential toys for any age are books, nature, and household items kids can use. A playroom full of toys is fun, but a stick outside will be the coolest thing ever for your one-year-old. Emily was obsessed with keys when she was one, so my mom went to our local hardware store and asked for discarded keys, and she used them to make Emily her very own set of keys. She carried those keys everywhere for months and even slept with them. Now, as an older child, she loves putting her keys into a purse to pretend she's a grown-up. A few dollars at a hardware store years ago have outlasted any other toy for her. Another fabulous kid-friendly activity at this age is the Tupperware drawer in your kitchen. For years I fought our kids' interest in rummaging through our kitchen Tupperware storage drawer, but it always seemed to draw them in no matter how thoroughly I had just organized it. Eventually, I gave in, and it became one of their favorite activities to this day. One-year-olds love to stack and sort items, so a Tupperware drawer is the thing of dreams for this age. My desire for order and organization almost kept my kids from enjoying one of the best sources of entertainment in our household.

Clothes at this age are all about function. The cuter the outfit, the larger the guaranteed mess. We purchased most of our clothes secondhand for our kids at this age because this is when kids start to wear their clothes *hard*. It was also when I stopped picking the battle of trying to keep every outfit perfect. We put nice clothes aside and had play clothes at the ready so the kids could get them stained or messy. If there was an occasion to wear something nice, we would pull it out, but the nice stuff wasn't in the everyday rotation. I'm definitely not advocating for your child to look messy all the time, but at this age, a mess is truly inevitable. Add this consideration into your capsule wardrobe planning so grass stains and paint prints don't ruin the fancy dress from Grandma.

Life with a one-year-old is loud, chaotic, dramatic, messy, and magical. They see everything for the first time and truly absorb what it is. Imagine looking closely at grass for the first time and having the opportunity to admire and feel it. To us, it seems mundane and obvious, but to a toddler, it's mind-blowing. These little minds are working overtime to develop and figure out how to communicate all they see. They are sponges at this age and will never learn at such a fast rate as they do during this year. Give them the freedom to explore and wander. To play with water and see what happens when it spills. To eat spaghetti with their hands and experience what getting really messy feels like. Use your home and the items in it to keep them safe while allowing them the chance to repeatedly practice their new skills or knowledge.

Capsule Wardrobe for Age One:

Warm Weather	Cold Weather
6 to 9 short-sleeve shirts (or dresses)	6 to 9 long-sleeve shirts
3 to 5 pairs of shorts	3 to 5 pairs of pants
5 to 7 pairs of jammies	5 to 7 pairs of jammies
2 sweaters	3 to 5 sweaters
2 swimsuits	1 or 2 coats

Diaper Bag Essentials for Age One:

- ► Mom's purse supplies
- ► 6 to 8 diapers and a pack of wipes
- ► Changing pad
- ► 2 or 3 spare outfits
- ► Hand sanitizer or cleaning wipes
- ► 2 or 3 travel toys or books
- ► Plastic trash bags and a wet-dry bag
- ► Snacks
- ► Water bottle
- ► First aid supplies

Household Essentials for Age One:

- ▶ Baby gates/child-proofing supplies
- ▶ Mats or modular play couch for indoor play
- ▶ Child-safe versions of household items like kitchen knives, cleaning supplies, keys, or TV remote
- ▶ Toddler-safe plates/cups/utensils
- ▶ Age-appropriate books
- ▶ A Tupperware drawer
- ▶ Clothes that can get messy
- ▶ Stain remover
- ▶ Toddler-friendly art supplies
- ▶ Rain/mud boots

Journal Prompts/Discussion Questions:

- ▶ Where are you getting your information for baby and one-year-old development?
- ▶ Is a nursery important to you?
- ▶ What consignment options are available for you to find or sell baby things?
- ▶ Do you have a plan for where to store unused baby equipment?

CHAPTER 10

AGES TWO AND THREE: SURVIVING THE TODDLER YEARS

Pick your battles.

L et's be real. Toddlerhood is probably one of the most talked about, dreaded, beloved, difficult, enjoyable, relatable, funny, and confusing stages of parenthood I've experienced so far. If I'm being honest, I would likely take a sleepless newborn over a toddler most days because by the time you get to this stage, the newborn days feel like a breeze compared to trying to convince a small human they should not eat the random French fry they found on the ground in the Target parking lot. This age can be challenging, but it's also where things get really exciting and fun as a parent. Yep, I said it, two- and three-year-olds are *fun*.

Life with toddlers is loud and fast. Your babbling little one-year-old has made the leap from those precious first steps to a real-life running, talking, full-fledged toddler who is rapidly absorbing all the information around them. They hardly ever walk anywhere and are always pushing the boundaries of safety—which is developmentally necessary for this age even if it also gives you your first gray hairs. Their language skills have exploded, and they likely have several hundred words in their vocabulary arsenal by this age. But they also have BIG feelings and don't always know how to share those feelings. (Hello, tantrums.) Gross motor skills have become more refined, and they are likely working on skills like jumping, tiptoeing, balancing, or riding a bike. Fine motor skills have become focused on things like learning to get dressed, feeding themselves with utensils, holding something to color with, or washing their hands.[13] The speed of life picks up the pace with kids this age, mostly because your kid can probably run really fast now.

As a parent, this stage of life is where you can build monumentally strong foundations for your family and your children. Independence is a constant desire for any child, but two- and three-year-olds live for it. "No Mommy, my do it!" was a phrase I heard on repeat with my kids at this age, and for a while, I still did my best to get whatever we were trying to accomplish done within my time frame and to my standards.

13 Deena Shin, "2 Year Old Milestones: Development, Growth, Speech, Language, and More," July 12, 2024, Huckleberry, https://huckleberrycare.com/blog/2-year-old-milestones-development-growth-speech-language-and-more; and Deena Shin, "3 Year Old Milestones: Development, Growth, Speech, Language, and More," September 17, 2024, Huckleberry, https://huckleberrycare.com/blog/3-year-old-milestones-development-growth-speech-language-and-more.

I finally learned how important "picking your battles" really is as a parent and that by allowing my kids to do more for themselves, they were honing their skills.

Each little opportunity for exerting independence became a matter of deciding whether to "pick the battle." If something wasn't morally or mortally threatening, then it was likely something I would let go of. This emphasized the times I would strongly say "no" and allowed our kids to develop remarkable independence from an early age. By the age of three, all four kids could get themselves ready for the day alone. They knew to put dirty laundry in the hamper, open their shutters, brush their teeth, and put on their shoes when it was time to leave. Sometimes as a parent, the best thing I did was to remove myself from their learning and let them figure it out (which goes against all my maternal instincts, by the way). I wanted to help but, in many cases, I was hindering my kids' ability to learn for themselves.

At this age, toddlers discover they have opinions and want to share them—often. They might desperately want to wear two different shoes or a princess tiara everywhere they go. All three of our daughters were *adamant* about picking out their clothes by this age, and with Emily, our oldest, I was not about to let that happen. Just as I had a hard time letting go of my precious home décor vignettes because I thought our house would not be pretty without them, I was concerned about the image I would be portraying as a mom if I let my child leave the house not dressed correctly. By the time Sophie and Maggie were toddlers, that ship had sailed for me. I had far bigger fish to fry, and I was too tired to worry about the fact that my independent-thinking two-year-old Sophie wanted to wear all the patterns in her winter wardrobe at once in the middle of the summer. Maggie went through a stage where she would only wear the same tutu. Every. Single. Day. If she couldn't wear this tutu, it wasn't a good outcome, so I became great at washing laundry every evening. Turns out kids can look adorable in mismatched or backward outfits too. Jay, on the other hand, had a strong distaste for clothes at this age, and there were many times we arrived at our destination . . . underdressed. The amount of pride my kids had from wearing an outfit they picked out and put on themselves was far more rewarding than winning the battle of wills when it came to clothing.

Remember that in chapter 6, we looked at clothes through the lens of function. This helped me immensely as we entered the toddler stage. It was OK when Jay wore only socks in the muddy backyard or when Sophie got paint on her pants at art class. Clothes are washable, and memories stay.

Our kids all became interested in the kitchen at this age, and yours might too. We used our kitchen as a place to discover, and I had to constantly remind myself that messes can always be cleaned up. It was another big lesson for me in removing myself from the learning opportunity. On many occasions, I would show someone how to do something and then try to micromanage them doing it properly. No toddler is going to cut a vegetable the correct way, yet it would drive me crazy to watch them do it incorrectly. I had to learn to manage my expectations and realize it was a "me problem." Our kids were having a blast participating in meal preparation, and my expectations for correctness or perfection were getting in the way of learning and enjoyment. I can't tell you how many eggshells I've pulled out of the pancake mix or how much flour my poor vacuum has had to clean up. But yet again, messes can always be cleaned up, while memories of little hands cracking eggs or adding ingredients will stay forever.

Remember when I told you about Emily and Sophie dumping out all the puzzle pieces from our game cabinet? They were two and three at the time, and it was the first time I started seeing that toys were no longer interesting to them and they had rounded the corner from babyhood into toddler-hood. They would enjoy picking something up and playing with it for a few minutes before moving on to something else and leaving my poor house (and sanity) in disarray. My house was a mess with discarded toys, and I couldn't understand why their favorite toys were no longer holding their attention. It turns out that toys haven't actually been around for that long.

Michaeleen Doucleff, author of *Hunt, Gather, Parent: What Ancient Cultures Can Teach Us About the Lost Art of Raising Happy, Helpful Little Humans*, shares that toys were a result of the Industrial Revolution and "burgeoning con-sumerism," not for the sake of childhood development or entertainment.[14] I'm sorry, come again? That's right; before

---

14 Michaeleen Doucleff, *Hunt, Gather, Parent: What Ancient Cultures Can Teach Us About the Lost Art of Raising Happy, Helpful Little Humans* (New York: Avid Reader Press, 2021).

the Industrial Revolution, no matter their age, location, or family's financial means, kids didn't have toys that had been purchased. They were creative with their surroundings and used random objects from inside and outside their homes to find ways to play. Dolls made of spare fabric from Mom's sewing basket. Swords made from sticks. Bits of nature used for pretend cooking. Play wasn't a priority for families, and toys didn't exist. Toys were created because for the first time, parents had more disposable income, *and* there were new methods to produce items in bulk. From the beginning of time—except for the last two hundred-odd years—kids played the same way. So how did we get from kids making dolls out of sticks and fabric to me cleaning up hundreds of puzzle pieces off my living room floor? Are toys bad? Absolutely not. But is it possible that in the last century or two, we've put a little too much emphasis on spending money on items to entertain our kids that happen to take up a lot of storage space in our homes? Possibly. So where does that leave us when it comes to keeping our very active two- and three-year-olds entertained? Toys may not have existed for very long, but for thousands of years kids of all ages, especially toddlers, have found ways to entertain themselves.

Toddlers live to explore their environments. Whether it's their closet, the kitchen, the backyard, the playroom, the car, or anywhere else, if they can see it, they want to explore it. Have you ever watched a toddler enter a new place? They enter with a little hesitancy, and then it's as if someone turns on their discover mode and they go *everywhere*. They want to touch everything, see each room, find the petty, look at all the toys, eat all the snacks, look under the couch, and then do it all again. One time we went to a friend's house for dinner, and while everyone was playing in the backyard, Maggie disappeared. We found her inside our friend's house looking through their fridge because she wanted to see "what they had in there."

Exploration is the key to entertainment at this age. If you're looking for ways to keep your toddler entertained, allow them to explore. Take them outside to wander around the yard (as you supervise from a distance). Let them play with mud and get really dirty. Give them a bowl of ice in the middle of summer and see what they do with it. Purchase an indoor climbing gym to develop their balance and grip strength. Just as when they were babies and one-year-olds, the key to keeping toddlers interested is to set them up for success by creating an environment where they can safely investigate their surroundings, especially outside. Toys are not the enemy, but you'll quickly find that a lot of times they will be discarded in place of something much simpler, like a flower or stick that offers more freedom for imaginative play. Toys and indoor play (even ones meant to foster creativity) have rules and a specific purpose. Inside, a doll will only be a doll. But outside, a pile of mulch can be any number of creative things: a fairy garden, a pie, or even the gateway to a magical land. Outside the walls of your home and your playroom, the rules of play fall away, and kids of all ages have the freedom to use their imaginations. This is the age when you might feel like you live outside your house more than indoors—and that's great!

When your kids are playing inside, keep plenty of books, art supplies, and building materials like MAGNA-TILES® or DUPLOS® handy. A chalkboard or easel can add entertainment time, as long as you make sure it's all washable. Paint is a wonderfully fun way to keep your kids busy, but definitely be prepared for cleanup. Invest in larger toy options for inside, like a modular play couch or an indoor swing to help get the wiggles out. I'm always a fan of a few larger items instead of a lot of toys with little pieces. Your child may find a few toys that they really love; however, more often than not, their interest in toys will evolve as they grow, but their desire to explore won't change for a long time.

Car Supplies for Toddlers

Toddlerhood is the start of the sweet spot for family adventures. You're no longer nap-trapped all day, so you have newfound freedom to get out of the house, but you might not be able to leave the house without supplies and backups. Potty accidents, spills, snacks, and muddy shoes are all real possibilities when you are a toddler parent, but instead of carrying everything in your diaper bag, you are now at the stage where a fully stocked car kit will be all you need for some fun on the go. I keep a bin in my trunk with all my car supplies so I can carry less on the go but still be prepared just in case. Over the years, my car supplies have evolved as our family's ages and needs have changed, but on any given day, you can bet my car is ready for a full-day adventure, even if we are just going to the grocery store.

Stroller wagon. Double strollers are a thing of the past, and stroller wagons are the way to go. Ask any parent with two or more young kids right now, and they will agree. Stroller wagons are now replacing the traditional double stroller among most parents these days (except for the double BOB because those will always be necessary for joggers). I wish we had gotten on this trend much sooner than we did. We purchased our VEER wagon just before Jay was born, and it completely changed our ability to go somewhere as a family. It lived in our trunk for years and was a remarkably reliable part of my car essentials.

Travel potty and liners. When we started potty training our kids, I did some research and came across the concept of a car potty. It was a potty insurance policy for us that has turned out to be one of the most used pieces of kid gear we've ever purchased. We have been to so many places where a potty wasn't available, and this little car potty has saved the day. During the height of COVID-19, we took a trip to the beach but didn't think about how most restaurants were closed. Thankfully, we were stocked with our car potty and able to safely make it to our destination without any incidents. I highly recommend having one of these.

Diapers, wipes, and changing pad. ALWAYS. Always. Always keep spare wipes and diapers in your car. I have learned this the hard way many times when I've accidentally forgotten to restock my diaper bag, we've had a longer than anticipated outing, or an especially messy diaper situation. Knowing there are extra diapers and wipes handy if we need them is such a reassurance when we venture out. Along with spare diapers and wipes, we keep a fully stocked portable changing pad for last minute grab-and-go diaper changes.

Spares of EVERYTHING. Yes, this seems a tad extreme, but I basically double everything I plan to bring and keep a second set in the car. I have spare grocery bags for messy clothes, dirty diapers, or whatever else we might need them for. I used to keep a spare outfit for each family member, but at this point we would need a bigger car to keep that many outfits handy, so now it's just the youngest ones plus a few random oversized T-shirts for someone to throw on just in case. I try to keep a few granola bars and bottles of water in my car supplies just in case of an emergency, but I find that these can be hard to remember to swap out so they aren't going bad.

Water-resistant picnic blanket/bag. Have you seen those picnic blankets that fold up into a bag? My mom got me one years ago, and I love how easily I can store it in the car and access it when we need it. I've used this blanket for lining the car when the dog is messy, an impromptu picnic, a clean place for diaper changes, and much more. It stores easily and doesn't take up much space, and the benefit of having it is awesome.

Paper towels and tissues. Kids inevitably bring messes, so having something to clean up those messes is always helpful. Every so often I will wait until a roll of paper towels is almost finished and put that roll in my car essentials kit. I usually keep a box of tissues in my front seat console and store the paper towels with the car potty or diaper supplies.

Waterproof car seat liner. Accidents happen, and when they do, we are ready with a waterproof car seat liner. When one of our kids is actively potty training, we keep this in their car seat all the time, and then once we feel confident in their potty skills, we keep it in our car basket. There are plenty of uses besides potty accidents such as muddy pants or eating meals on the road and not wanting the car seat to get dirty. This liner is washable and way easier to clean than the entire car seat.

First aid kit. It's always a smart idea to keep basic first aid with you wherever you go with kids. It's especially helpful to have extra first aid supplies in your car for those boo-boos that happen on the go. I have relied on our car first aid countless times on the road, including family trips where we needed extras of something I didn't pack in our suitcases. Key items to have on hand include antibiotic ointment, Band-Aids* in multiple sizes, pain relievers for all ages, and instant ice packs.

Let's Choose Less grew from our family's desire for simplicity, yet I was overcomplicating even the smallest of decisions when it came to parenting. It's one thing to have a decluttered kitchen, but having a kitchen that allows all family members to actively participate changes the entire dynamic and purpose of the space. When you look at your home and your belongings through the lens of a toddler, you begin to see how overwhelming, fun, exciting, and engaging things can be. The kitchen becomes a magical place to learn and spend time with grown-ups. The yard is a wonderland of new ways to play. Each part of your home is an opportunity for play when you begin to reshape your view. Once I learned how to slow down and give our kids room to safely explore, I realized how much extra pressure I had been adding to all of us. Playtime isn't supposed to be stressful, and I was taking away the fun by looking at it as a grown-up instead of a kid. Jon and I learned how to let our kids live *with us*—not just near us—by opening ourselves to the idea that our toddlers' desire for independence and exploration was their way of telling us they were trying to learn.

Capsule Wardrobe for Ages Two and Three:

Warm Weather	Cool/Cold Weather
6 to 9 short-sleeve shirts (or dresses)	6 to 9 long-sleeve shirts (or dresses)
3 to 5 pairs of shorts 2 or 3 pairs of under dress shorts for girls	3 to 5 pairs of pants
3 to 5 pairs of jammies	3 to 5 pairs of jammies
2 sweaters/cardigans	3 to 5 sweaters/sweatshirts
2 swimsuits	1 or 2 coats
Shoes (tennis shoes, waterproof shoes, rain boots)	Play shoes (tennis shoes, winter boots)

A raincoat and a good set of rain boots are great for this age.

Diaper Bag Essentials for Ages Two and Three:

- ► Mom's purse supplies
- ► 4 diapers and a pack of wipes
- ► Changing pad
- ► 1 or 2 spare outfits
- ► Hand sanitizer or cleaning wipes
- ► 1 to 3 travel toys or books
- ► Plastic trash bags and a wet-dry bag
- ► Snacks
- ► Water bottle
- ► First-aid supplies

Household Essentials for Ages Two and Three:

- ► Baby gates/child-proofing supplies
- ► Mats or modular couch for indoor play
- ► Child-safe versions of household items like kitchen knives, cleaning supplies, keys, or TV remote
- ► Age-appropriate books
- ► Clothes that can get messy
- ► Stain remover
- ► Toddler-friendly art supplies
- ► Rain/mud boots
- ► Waterproof shoes
- ► Chalk
- ► Bathroom step stool
- ► Faucet extender
- ► Potty seat

Journal Prompts/Discussion Questions:

▶ What is an area of your home or life you currently have or anticipate having trouble relinquishing control?

▶ What is a battle you are willing to pick and what is something that isn't a big deal to you?

▶ What part of your childhood home do you have the most memories spending time in?

CHAPTER 11

AGES FOUR AND FIVE: ENCOURAGING INDEPENDENCE

Give them time.

There's a special threshold waiting for every parent at their child's fourth birthday. It is the line where kids get a little easier. Yes, every part of parenting is still hard, but in our house, turning four was when things started to get a little less challenging. Diapers are officially a thing of the past, and you'll finally be able to go on bigger and longer adventures, with less stuff to carry. If you've played your cards right, your child might be able to get dressed and ready for their day independently, help with household chores and younger siblings, play for longer periods without needing parental involvement, and be responsible for a lot of their belongings. Yes, seriously! And all of this starts around the age of four. By the time they are cruising into age five, life will be drastically different from the chaotic toddler days, and you might even begin to forget about some of the difficulties that you faced during those years (keyword: *might*).

Developmental milestones for four- and five-year-olds are just plain fun. They can run farther, jump higher, stir up more mischief, and move faster than ever before. They start to learn their letters and may even begin reading. Kids at this age might develop a deep love for a particular activity or find they have a special talent. Their interest in learning will be sparked by things that will seem new all over again. Stories you read when they were babies may come back into the rotation but with new meaning and questions. The alphabet will present new opportunities to make connections, when before it was just a fun song to sing together. Crayons can be used for doodling but also for tracing, writing, coloring in the lines, or creating new masterpieces. You will be able to pass the soccer ball back and forth, run around playing tag, and enjoy board games together. Their independence will astound you, but it also will test you. They will think they can do far more than you might want them to, so you'll have to make the "choose your battle" decision frequently. I struggled with letting our kids decide when they were prepared for something instead of when the books, websites, and blogs said they should.

Kids of all ages have opinions, but four- and five-year-olds can use a *small* amount of rationality to share their thoughts. Sophie didn't want to play soccer for years despite the pressure from her well-meaning Mom. After years of watching Emily play, much to our surprise, one day five-year-old Sophie declared she wanted to join a soccer team as well. She was finally able to explain to us that she likes to know what will happen with something before she does it, so all those seasons of watching Emily helped her understand what to expect with soccer. The lightbulb flashed for me, and I finally understood my daughter on a deeper level. Sophie never did things unless it was on her own time, and it had been a huge cause of frustration for me. But now I was able to see that she's the kind of person who likes to read the end of the book before she reads the whole thing. Talk about a parenting revelation! This may not always be the case for your four- or five-year-old, but I'm willing to bet that if you ask them for some reasoning, they will likely be able to provide their thought process, and this may help you understand each other a little better.

At this age, the best thing you can give your child is time. Whether it's time to freely explore outside, time sitting with you and listening to a story, time to try a new recipe in the kitchen, or time to learn how to fold laundry, four- and five-year-olds thrive with quality time from their grown-ups. As Maria Montessori wisely said, "Play is the work of a child." Play can be defined in many ways, but to kids, it usually falls under the categories of helping or being around others. Focus your energy on spending as much time as you can looking your child in the eyes and engaging with them. A new toy is fun, but doing a puzzle with Mom is way better. Now that you can go for longer, bigger adventures, start to find common interests and wholly embrace them. There will be time for activities and busyness in the future, but these precious years are when you can solidify your family values in your child's heart. At age four, Maggie's favorite thing in the world is to snuggle. I know she won't always want to do this, so when she crawls into my lap and asks to snuggle and read, you better believe we're going to do it.

This is when you will start to see some of your hard, foundational *Let's Choose Less* work come to fruition. Parenting is innately tough, but there are varying levels of difficulty. The smaller your child is, the more physical struggles you have, such as carrying an infant car seat, a diaper bag, and an unhappy toddler across a parking lot. As your child ages, the parenting predicaments become more mental and emotional, like when you've been asked for a snack one thousand times in an hour or can't pretend to be Thomas the Train for another minute. Once you reach the four- and five-year-old stages, your challenges will present differently than they likely ever have in your parenting journey so far. You'll be answering questions that seem to always be asked at the most inconvenient of times—such as "How do babies come out of your tummy?" while in the middle of family dinner. Or "Who made God?" while changing a blowout diaper.

Your own physical challenges of parenting shift too. This stage was when I was finally able to get treatment for my diastasis recti and back pain after not needing to lift or hold my kids all day long. It's when I rediscovered sleep and the ability to sit down. It's when I began voraciously reading character development books and realized how often I was mindlessly scrolling on my phone to mentally check out. It's also when your family begins to prepare for the transition into elementary school, which can stir up emotions for everyone.

Currently, while I write this chapter in our home office, we are homeschooling our oldest kids. This wasn't always our plan. We explored many different education options and even had a full year of public school before coming to this lifestyle. I have no idea what the future will bring for us when it comes to our kids' education, but I learned in our early elementary school research that there is no right answer *and* that answer may be different for each child. You might feel like whatever choice you make is one that will determine the rest of your child's life, but I'm here to reassure you that all you can do is make the best decision you can with the information you currently have.

Chores for Four- and Five-Year-Olds

Chores as we view them through adult eyes are completely different than how our kids see them. Household responsibilities present kids with opportunities for independence, the chance to be an active and participating family member, and more time to spend with someone they love. To us, chores are drudgery because we have been doing them for so long and would much rather be drinking coffee and curling up with a good book. To our kids, these tasks are new and exciting. Chores offer them the chance to help, work with you, and feel grown-up.

At the ages of four and five, children can perform many household tasks without help. They may not be performed

perfectly, but they will give your child the chance to con-
tribute to the household and claim ownership over a certain
aspect of the family responsibilities. By four or five years old,
kids can be massively helpful when it comes to work around
the house. Let me be clear that I'm not going to tell you to
teach your kids how to do everything so you don't have to do
it. This is the part where you spend time together, taking care
of your home—*together*. Kids will always be kids, so some
days this will work far better than others, but overall, we have
watched our kids develop pride in their ability to care for
our home alongside us. If you want your kids to be able to
help, you must give them the chance to try. There are very
few times throughout the day that our kids are not involved
in our household tasks. From an early age, they helped sort
laundry, cleared their plates from the table, participated in
meal preparation, cleared up toys, and unloaded the dishwasher. Even a toddler can sort out the silverware drawer! If
you have not allowed your child to be involved in the chore
process before, start small and then work your way to larger
tasks. Something as simple as being responsible for making
their bed each morning or putting their dirty laundry in
the right location will still offer them the opportunity to
be a contributing family member. Plus it's one less bed for
you to make!

We have included our kids in every aspect of our
household tasks since they could pick up an item. Maggie
was unloading plates from the dishwasher when she was less
than two, Sophie has always loved sorting laundry, Emily is

amazing in the kitchen, and Jay likes to line up all his cars or garbage trucks on the shelf. Now that they are older, our kids willingly come to help or ask to be involved because they care about taking care of our home as much as we do. No one is ever as surprised as I am when I turn the corner to see our kids tidying without asking, but that's because it's never been presented as something to loathe; it's just a part of living in our home and being a member of our family.

Chore List

- ▶ Empty the dishwasher
- ▶ Sort laundry/put laundry away
- ▶ Make beds
- ▶ Tidy up
- ▶ Put toys/books away
- ▶ Set the table
- ▶ Clear dishes from the table
- ▶ Throw trash away
- ▶ Dust/vacuum/mop
- ▶ Pull weeds
- ▶ Feed pets
- ▶ Help mix ingredients in the kitchen
- ▶ Water plants
- ▶ Wash dishes in the sink

Things I'm Not Afraid to Get Rid of

We were hosting a big family dinner at our house, and Emily, who is usually the life of the party, was suddenly hysterical. She hardly could get the words out between her broken sobs: "No, I'm not hurt. But I'm really afraid Mommy will be mad at me."

It turns out she was playing and left a massive series of scratches on our coffee table. (For the record, our coffee table is something I found at an antique store before we got married and then decided to try my hand at "DIY.") It's ugly, the paint is chipping, one leg is wobbly, and there's a sticky spot that never seems to get un-sticky. It's truly not nice or fancy at all. I couldn't believe Emily was so worried about this after all the times we had told our kids that "things can always be replaced" and "we care more about you than stuff." For whatever reason, at this moment she had forgotten all of it and was terrified she had destroyed a perfectly good (in her mind) coffee table and was about to be in big trouble. Before I could respond, my sister laughingly said, "Emily, when has your mom ever cared about stuff more than you?" Sweet Emily's smile broke through her tears, and she giggled while responding, "Never!" My relief was instant that our daughter could laugh at the fact that her mom truly doesn't place value on items over her children. Do we let our kids wreck everything in our home? Absolutely not. But this doesn't mean we aren't afraid to replace or get rid of items that are no longer needed. That coffee table had been on my list to replace for a while, but kids are irreplaceable.

At the ages of four and five, your kids will have a new awareness of "things." They may realize when they damage something and feel guilty for it. They start to take ownership of certain items such as small gifts they get from the treasure box at school or those really fun toys that come in the kids' meal bags. Collections and treasures start to accumulate in random piles in your home, garage, yard, car, pockets, and anywhere else they can find a place to stash them. It's the perfect age to start showing your kiddos how to take active responsibility for their things and when it's time to let go of certain items. As a parent, it's your job to set the example and let go of items when they no longer serve a purpose in your home. If you are encouraging your child to pare down their rock collection, it's only fair that they see you doing the same with your things as well. If you aren't quite prepared to compare an overabundant Polly Pocket collection in your daughter's closet to the shoe collection in your closet, an excellent place to pare down in your home is items that do not give you anxiety about parting with.

I originally titled this section "Things I'm Not Afraid to Throw Away," but it felt too intense and frankly not very environmentally friendly. There are piles of things in your home where you can trim off the excess without having to fully commit to a major downsize or purge. You'll find them in your sock drawer, on your kitchen counter, or anywhere that dust might be collecting. Look for items that will help your home feel lighter while also setting the example for your whole family that just because something entered your home doesn't mean it has to live there for good. Set a timer and take a lap around your house to pick up any items you have sitting out and no longer need. Get the kids involved and make it into a game. (Who can carry the most?) Once you have your items, then you can decide where they go, as long as it's out of your home. Don't be afraid to get rid of the birthday party favors congregating under the couch, the excess paperwork on your counter, the princess dress that leaves glitter all over your carpet, or the shoes your son grew out of a year ago. While a major closet purge always feels good, this is your opportunity to skim the surface for all the extra little things our eyes tend to skip over. Use this as a chance to show your kids that your home's value comes from the people within, not from the items. Sometimes the best way to teach is to model the behavior, so if your child happens to love collecting something, it might be because you have shown them how.

Broken toys. I know a lot of families will repair toys once they inevitably break, but I am very particular about what toys we choose to repair. Most of the time, if it's small, plastic, or noisy, once it breaks, we say goodbye. Anything wood, open-ended, or sentimental, we make every effort to fix. We rarely miss a toy once it's gone, and parting with the broken ones can help reduce toy clutter.

Anything with glitter. I have a thing about glitter . . . I can't stand it. So anything that comes into our house covered in glitter will quickly make its way right back out. Once glitter is around, it never goes away. So, no glitter.

Food that is questionable. Depending on the food, I draw the line at a few days for raw meat, a week for produce, and a week for leftovers. If something is still in the fridge by that point, I will toss it. I also try to reduce food sharing where possible to prevent germs, so I typically don't eat the kid's leftovers.

Excess or random artwork. School paperwork builds up like crazy. Add in all the extra art projects, pictures, and notes that accumulate, and the paper clutter can get out of control in one afternoon. As I've mentioned, I have one zippered pouch for each child to hold their art, sentimental school projects, and other paperwork for the school year. If the pouch gets too full, there's too much inside. Everything else gets tossed at some point. A lot of times I'll keep a stack on the counter that the kids will add to throughout the week. When the stack gets too high, or at the end of the week, we sort through and get rid of things together.

Stained clothes. I'm at the point in my parenting journey where some clothes are just not worth the effort to try and save. If there's a onesie that's been the casualty of a massive blowout, I don't save it. An old T-shirt with spaghetti sauce? Not worth it. Most of my kids' clothes are hand-me-downs, so it's not a shame when they get ruined. I keep a few nice outfits that are not play clothes for each kid, and everything else is fair game.

Missing socks. Y'all, don't tell my mom about this one! I used to keep a bag full of mismatched socks to try to find matches, and it would drive me crazy. I would try so hard to find the matches, but no matter how many matches I made, the bag never seemed to be less empty. Now, if a sock is mismatched for too long, it just goes away. Plus, our kids grow out of socks so fast it usually doesn't matter anyway. If you aren't ready to part with the sock that is missing, you can always put its match to use as a cleaning rag.

Packaging. Are you someone who decants? I love that word. It's just a fancy way of saying you take things out of the store packaging and put them into another space-saving container. We shop in bulk, so a lot of the products we purchase come in bulk-size packaging. Cardboard takes up a lot of space, so by removing the packing, we eliminate a ton of excess clutter. If we put all the granola bars in a bin, we can reduce having a big box for only a few bars. I also do not keep the original packaging for *every* toy we own. I know that if the toy is really used, we won't need the box to store it in. Shoeboxes, diaper boxes, Amazon boxes, and all kinds of other packaging can stack up, so it's a constant effort to fight that clutter and keep it out of the house.

Old shoes. At any given time, my kids own about four pairs of shoes each. For four kids, four pairs of shoes each that they outgrow every season means we have a lot of spare shoes lying around. If a pair is worn through, it's time to let it go. I keep those that are in good condition if I can and donate the rest.

Since Maggie is our youngest daughter, I donate a lot of her shoes as she grows out of them if they aren't ones Jay will wear.

I do not throw everything away, contrary to what my friends might think. I am, however, always on the lookout for things we don't need to keep. I accept that our time with certain items has finished and it's time for that item to leave our home. There are some things I have a hard time parting with, like baby clothes that have emotional attachments or anything with a handprint on it, but I can easily discard paperwork, ruined clothes, or old food. This practice has worn off on our kids, though, and now they willingly will ask to donate or discard items that no longer fit, serve a purpose, or they don't need.

It's important to note that at this age, kids may begin to have their own collections of special things. In our home, we encourage autonomy for our kids over caring for our belongings and make sure there's a dedicated spot for precious items to go. If a collection becomes too big for the designated storage location, it's time to pare down.

In the end, I always want our kids to feel like I choose them over stuff. If I want them to believe it, I need to show them! I could have easily been angry with Emily for scratching our coffee table, but instead, I hugged her and told her it was OK to make a mistake. Things are just things, after all, and they can always be replaced.

Ages four and five mark the start of a new stage for you and your child. Your adorable little baby has become an independent, helpful, inquisitive person. They went from being your squishy, tantrum-prone toddler to a curious preschooler in the blink of an eye. (And they somehow made this transition right before you!) As our kids evolve, so do we as parents. I am not the same parent I was a year ago, three years ago, and certainly not eight years ago. Each stage of parenting brings us new growth opportunities, but the snuggles are always just as sweet. Embrace the time answering questions, playing in the garden, learning new skills side by side, and caring for your home together. Because before you know it, your kids will change and grow again.

Capsule Wardrobe for Ages Four and Five:

Warm Weather	Cool/Cold Weather
6 to 9 short-sleeve shirts (or dresses)	6 to 9 long sleeve-shirts (or dresses)
3 to 5 pairs of shorts	3 to 5 pairs of pants
5 to 7 pairs of jammies	5 to 7 pairs of jammies
2 sweaters	3 to 5 sweaters
2 swimsuits	1 or 2 coats
Shoes (tennis shoes, wet shoes, rain boots)	Shoes (tennis shoes, winter boots)

Journal Prompts/Discussion Questions:

▶ What is your earliest memory?

▶ What is something you weren't allowed to do as a kid that you are planning to let your children do?

▶ Did you have a favorite activity when you were little?

▶ What book do you remember being read to you as a child?

▶ What was the first household chore you were responsible for?

▶ What is one thing you know you should throw away but are afraid to get rid of?

PART FOUR

LET'S CHOOSE LESS
ON PURPOSE

CHAPTER 12

TRAVEL

Do with less while away.

T he very first time I traveled as a parent was about four months after Emily, our oldest, was born. It was a last-minute decision to make the trek to Pennsylvania in the middle of winter for the funeral of a close family member. We didn't want to miss it, but we were also immensely intimidated by the prospect of traveling with our four-month-old, especially since we were still so new to parenting. We only had a day or two to make our plans before it was time to depart.

Our plan was hilariously complicated. As former residents of Pennsylvania, we had some friends who still lived in the area who had yet to meet Emily, so I took advantage of the opportunity for a quick visit. Emily and I boarded a flight together a day before Jon drove up to meet us for the funeral. We flew to the Philadelphia airport, followed by two different trains, then walked three-quarters of a mile (in the middle of the winter) to make it to our friend's house. For one overnight and our day of travel, I packed a full-size suitcase, a full-size stroller, a fully stocked diaper bag, a baby carrier, and four-month-old Emily. The kindness of strangers helped me as I boarded our flight, but it became glaringly obvious when we boarded our train how much stuff I had brought with us. I couldn't get all of our gear onto the train while also babywearing Emily, so I held up the train to get it all loaded. I was in trouble with the conductor for having a stroller on the train, and there was no room for us to fit into a seat because it was rush hour. We uncomfortably blocked the walkway with all our things for the hourlong train ride while Emily slept peacefully in her baby carrier. When we arrived at our destination, I was completely exhausted.

The following day, Jon had driven almost ten hours by himself to meet us and transport us farther north for the funeral. We made multiple trips to unload the car into our hotel room for our two-night stay. In addition to all the things we had packed ourselves, the sweet friends we visited had toys and clothes to send home with us. In all my packing preparation, I forgot to check the weather. The funeral took place in the middle of a snowstorm, and neither Emily nor I were dressed appropriately. We spent the entire funeral in the car and were only able to attend the reception indoors afterward. She and I entered the reception to many comments of "Oh, I didn't realize you were here!" After saying our goodbyes and picking up an extra passenger to come home with us for a few days, we squished into the car again and began the long drive home. Emily was beyond exhausted and over being in her car seat, and she let us know by screaming for at least half of the drive. We stopped more than anticipated, this being our first car trip with a baby, and the drive ended up taking much longer. By the time we got home, I swore I was never going to travel again. Eventually I was brave enough to try again, but I'll never forget my baptism by fire first attempt to travel as a parent.

As we began pursuing a life of less things at home, I realized we could also live with less while traveling. With each trip we took, I would take notes to see what we brought and what we didn't need. I repeatedly realized I was overpacking, and it became a game for me to see how little I could get away with taking on our trips. I learned that just like having a plan for where everything went and a purpose for each item at home, the same mindset applied to travel. Eventually we created a system for packing and decision-making for trips. We kept detailed lists of what we packed, what we ate, and we adjusted our notes as our trips progressed. We acquired gear that was adaptable for all kinds of travel, and we learned that investing in one very nice piece of gear could eliminate many smaller, less expensive items.

Trying to travel with a stroller was always a huge dilemma. We knew we needed one, but there wasn't always room to bring one. A big purchase we made was our VEER wagon. The VEER eliminated our need for transporting a bulky stroller and also filled the requirement of being able to transport things along with multiple kids. Add the helpful feature that it folded flat and took up less room in our trunk than a stroller, and we were sold.

As a large family, especially with young kids, it's always more cost-effective and less stressful to travel with most of our food (if we are driving). The day before we leave, we usually stock up at Costco and then transport a majority of our food with us. We used to pack multiple coolers that did a subpar job of keeping our food fresh until we invested in a YETI cooler. It fits perfectly in the back of our minivan and is able to hold so much food. We eliminated the need for multiple coolers with just one reliable one.

Over and over, we evaluated what we were using and asked ourselves if there was a more efficient way. The more kids we had, the less we were able to bring, so we had to be strategic in what was necessary for the time we would be away. Most of the time we drive because flying with a family of six is not appealing to us or our bank account, so my travel mindset usually involves a car, but if you're a family of flyers, these ideas can easily be adapted for plane travel. The first step in traveling with kids is to plan ahead. Check the weather, anticipate when you might need specialized equipment, evaluate what baby gear you might need, such as a stroller or high chair, and play the game of determining what you can do without. What you pack for your trip can make a huge difference in how prepared you feel. How prepared you feel upon departure can set the tone for your entire trip. Each trip is different, and just like packing your diaper bag, pack with your destination in mind.

Planning ahead can make or break your trip. Start a packing list and modify it for each trip. Remember that most times you'll have access to a store to purchase something you may have forgotten, so it's more important to prioritize the most vital things, like a beloved stuffed animal or a sound machine your kids can't sleep without.

Clothing

Just like every other part of parenting, traveling with kids is all about mindset. Less is more and can make a big difference in the happiness levels of all family members involved. If you're staying somewhere with a washing machine, plan to rewear outfits and do laundry midtrip to cut down on what you pack. It also never hurts to return home with clean laundry.

For any given trip, I use capsule packing for everyone. I create a formula depending on where we go and then let the kids pack which outfits they'd like to wear within my guidelines. For a family beach trip where I know we will be doing laundry, I will write out a packing list specifically to give to our kids, and then they can pack themselves. I use the same formula for myself, and a lot of times we switch out T-shirts and shorts for a dress or two. By creating a formula for everyone to use, I make less work for myself when it comes to packing clothes and giving my kids parameters for their own packing. This is usually something that happens around age four in our house. Whether we are headed to the beach or a mountain camping trip, before we pack a single item of clothing, we write out our capsule formula. Setting guidelines in advance streamlines the packing process and hopefully prevents overpacking.

Example beach trip clothes for one week of travel:

- ▶ 2 pairs of PJs
- ▶ 2 bathing suits
- ▶ 1 cover-up
- ▶ 3 T-shirts that can be matched with 3 pairs of shorts
- ▶ Tennis shoes
- ▶ Sandals

Packing Cubes

I never pack without packing cubes. As we had more kids, it became super challenging to remember which bag had a particular kid's clothes in it, and I also found that multiple bags added to logistical challenges when traveling. Each of our family members has a set of packing cubes in a specific color. Depending on the trip, we may only use one cube per family member and pack all the cubes in one bin or bag. I typically use an oversized bag for all our packing cubes if we are driving because it's more flexible to pack around harder items like a cooler. When we fly, I can fit everything in one big suitcase. When we arrive at our destination, I put each person's cube in their designated room. The kids know which color their cube is, and they can find their belongings easily versus having to dig through a shared bag. Now that our kids are older, the packing cube system has been great for teaching them to limit the number of items they pack and encouraging them to take care of their belongings while we are away. Once we return home, our older kids unpack their cubes themselves, which cuts down on reentry work for me.

Toiletries and First Aid

For years, I've struggled with how to transport toiletries and medicine. We all use mostly the same products, so it feels redundant to pack small individual sets of things when I know the kids' stuff will end up in the same bathroom as ours. To conserve space and mental energy, I started putting all our toiletries and medical supplies into one bag or bin. I keep individual items separated by Ziploc bags or toiletry bags, but it helps to keep it all in one easily moveable bag or bin. When we arrive at our destination, we determine which bathroom everyone will be using and place our supplies there. Everyone knows where all the toothbrushes, hairbrushes, self-care products, sunscreen, aloe, medicine, and whatever else we may have packed are located. We create a home base that makes everything easier to find and gives things a better chance of making it home again. We always have a small first aid kit, a travel thermometer, kid's Tylenol, adult Tylenol, and kid's Benadryl on hand. (And we know that most times if we need additional medications, we will be able to find a store or pharmacy nearby.) There have been many middle-of-the-night travel circumstances when I was very glad to have Tylenol on hand.

Kitchen Supplies

If we're going somewhere with a kitchen and we are driving, I pack my kitchen bin. It's a trick I learned from my mom that makes traveling with kids a breeze. As mentioned earlier, we travel with a lot of our own food and rarely eat out, so finding a place with a kitchen is usually at the top of my travel priorities. Most rentals with kitchens have some basic supplies, but over the years I've learned there's always something missing. I started to piece together a kitchen supply bin that could supplement what we might need. I have travel cutting boards, an old frying pan, a spatula, my own dish towels, paper plates, kid-friendly cups, tin foil, dish soap, and more in our bin. Whether it's a beach vacation, a mountain cabin, or a campground, this bin makes feeding our small army easy. I bring it on girl's trips and Jon brings it camping with his buddies, and every time there's something we need inside. It takes up room in our car, but I have never regretted bringing it. We've even been able to make meals at rest stops thanks to our cooler and kitchen bin. Obviously, if you're flying, this isn't something you'll pack, but I encourage you to consider it when driving.

For nonperishable food, I use a cardboard box. I have tried bringing items in other bags or bins, but a cardboard box always works the best because you can get rid of it when you've emptied your food supply (although I have yet to have that happen, thanks to a husband who loves to shop at Costco).

Toys

If you're looking for one guaranteed area to pack less, this is it. When you travel, get creative with the toys you choose to bring. Often, most of the toys you pack won't be used, so pack accordingly. If you're flying, you'll have to be even more creative. We never go on a trip without books. We pack books that have multiple stories in them to have less to keep track of and also so we don't have to read the same two stories the entire time we're gone. As our kids have gotten older, we've found that audiobooks are the best car entertainment for our family. We get prerecorded books from the library to listen to on headphones or play through the car speakers. If you choose to travel with an iPad, you can download books to read digitally and pack even less.

Since the focus of this book is ages zero to five, I suggest packing things to entertain that are also potentially disposable. A box of Band-Aids® or a new sticker book can go a long way with most little kids. Coloring supplies are fun at any age, so stocking up on a new set of crayons and a new coloring book may provide hours of entertainment. A cookie tray and magnets or toy cars won't take up a lot of space and can keep little minds occupied. Because our youngest, Jay, hates car trips, we always try to schedule a drive during his nap so we can buy ourselves some guaranteed time to make progress.

I keep a bag of travel toys hidden in our front hall closet with items our kids only see when we travel. It has puzzles, coloring supplies, travel toys, and anything new I might want

to add for an upcoming trip. One bag of toys for four kids—
and usually it's still too much. Take the opportunity to talk
to your kids, play games, have a sing-along, or appreciate the
scenery with your kids. Toys are awesome, but sometimes they
aren't a necessity, and when you travel, this is where you can
pare down significantly. But whatever you do, don't forget
their lovey or favorite stuffy! (And also, snacks. *All the snacks.*)

Sleep

Our kids are not reliable sleepers. They never have been and
may never be. Sleep has always been one of our biggest challenges on the road and at home. We never travel without
at least one night-light because I know we will inevitably
be awake overnight trying to sleepily maneuver through an
unfamiliar environment to find whoever is awake. I place
a night-light in the main hallway or in a bathroom I know will
be used overnight to save everyone from hurting themselves
or using overhead lights. If we are driving, I pack our sound
machines from home that have built-in night-lights, which
help replicate our kid's sleep environments and block out extra
ambient noise. We also have smaller travel sound machines
that take up less space, but our kids always tell us they aren't as
awesome as the ones from home.

Always check with your destination ahead of time to see
if there's a travel crib or pack-n-play available for your use,
especially if you're flying. If you are traveling with family, it
might be helpful to check with them and see if they could
bring anything with them. There have been multiple trips

where my in-laws or my parents have kindly transported a pack-n-play for us so we had more room in our car. If you're going to visit someone, it's helpful to talk in advance about what gear they might be able to have once you're there. When Emily and I took our inaugural trip together, I packed everything but a place for her to sleep at our friend's house. My friend had a pack-n-play for us to use, thankfully, because otherwise I wouldn't have put it past myself to try and bring one with me. If you have a kid of potty training age, it might be a good idea to pack an extra waterproof mattress cover just in case. If you child is learning how to sleep in a bed instead of a crib, it might be important to pack an extra bed rail to ensure their safety overnight.

I know many people try to replicate their home sleeping environment as much as possible when traveling, but it's just not always feasible. One of the best things I've found is to make sure that everyone is active during the day and ready for a good night's sleep. If our kids have pent-up energy, they are more likely to have a worse night's sleep than if they are exhausted. Also realistic expectations can mean everything when it comes to sleep and travel. Expect to have a rocky first night and anticipate that you may not have as thorough of a night's sleep as you would at home. But don't let that stop you from getting out and having fun. The more we travel, the better our kids get at sleeping in new environments.

Packing for a trip with kids is a little like a giant jigsaw puzzle. Adjust according to where you're going and what you may be doing. You know your family best, so if there's something that would make a big difference for one of your family members, it may be helpful to make room for it. On one trip, Emily wanted to be sure we brought our pencil sharpener for her colored pencils. Normally I wouldn't pack something so un-useful and random, but she *loves* coloring with colored pencils, so it was a big deal for her to be able to sharpen them, and she was so glad to have a pencil sharper with her. Each trip is different, and as your kids age, your packing list will evolve as well. It's fun to see what you grow out of or what items make it onto the list that didn't the last time you traveled.

Packing can be a painful task, or it can be fun. Having a packing list has helped make preparing for a trip much easier, and it keeps my focus on the exciting vacation ahead instead of stressing about what to bring.

Family Vacation Packing List Ideas:

Bed:

- ► Sound machine
- ► Night-light
- ► Pack-n-play with sheets
- ► Extra waterproof mattress cover
- ► Wipes/diapers
- ► Bedtime books
- ► Clothes, bathing suits, and jammies for each family member

Bath:

- Toiletries
- Razor
- Toothbrushes
- Hair detangler
- Kids shampoo/conditioner
- Soap
- Extra toilet paper
- First aid
- Kids Benadryl
- Kids Tylenol
- Aloe
- Thermometer

Outdoor:

- Beach toys
- Bubbles
- Stroller (if necessary)
- Sunscreen
- Floaties
- Towels
- Beach bag
- Kids sunglasses
- Kids shoes (tennis, water, play)
- Baby carrier/backpack (in exchange for a stroller)

Kitchen:

- ► High chair
- ► Eating utensils
- ► Cups
- ► Reusable water bottles
- ► Dishwasher detergent
- ► Dish soap
- ► Knife
- ► Cutting board
- ► Frying pan
- ► Baking sheet
- ► Any small amounts of spices we may need for meals we've planned
- ► Spatula
- ► Tin foil, plastic wrap, Ziplock bags

Other:

- ► Chargers
- ► Toys
- ► Art supplies
- ► Laundry detergent
- ► Books

LET'S CHOOSE LESS
PACKING TIPS:

▶ Keep an ongoing packing list to refer to and modify each time you travel.

▶ Identify what items are essential for your destination.

▶ Plan meals and grocery lists in advance.

▶ Invest in gear that will help your travel be more efficient.

▶ Use packing cubes to keep family members' clothes organized.

▶ Use one toiletry bag or bin to minimize products you travel with.

▶ Choose the toys you travel with wisely.

▶ Anticipate sleep challenges in advance.

Journal Prompts/Discussion Questions:

▶ What is one thing you can't leave behind when you travel?

▶ Is there a piece of gear you could invest in to make it easier to travel as a family?

▶ What is one thing you brought on your last trip that was unnecessary?

▶ What is something you left at home that you wished you had packed on your last trip?

CHAPTER 13

CELEBRATIONS

Gifts should not be the focus.

Every Christmas morning when I was a kid, we had two rules: don't go downstairs before anyone else, and meet in Mom and Dad's room first. As my sisters and I woke up, eager with anticipation, we would crawl into bed with our parents and wait until it was acceptable to wake whoever was still asleep and then venture downstairs. My sisters and I would excitedly wait at the top of the stairs while my parents went down to turn lights on, poured themselves a well-deserved cup of coffee, and got the video camera ready. Only then were we permitted to come down. It was a flurry of feet on the stairs, with our matching pajamas and shrieks of glee. We would eat chocolate for breakfast and ogle our stockings while Christmas music played on the speakers and coffee cake cooled on the stove. We were allowed to stay in our pajamas as long as we wanted to and would spend almost the whole day together in the family room opening and playing with our gifts, watching movies, and eating way too much candy.

Birthdays were no different. My mom took a cake decorating class to be able to make fun, party-themed cakes that are still the stuff of legends. I have relied on my mom's expert cake skills many times in my own parenting experience, and my kids still talk about the cakes or cupcakes she's made. Whether it's a surprise visit at school with a homemade treat, lunch from Chick-fil-A in a crowded cafeteria, a special experience, a favorite meal, or even just a birthday balloon to tie on your backpack, my mom always knows exactly what makes each of her kids feel special. For instance, on one of my birthdays in college, I was getting ready to celebrate when I received a knock on my dorm room door. My parents and sisters had driven two hours to surprise me with a birthday cake in hand. When you have a birthday in our family, everyone makes you feel special, especially my mom.

My childhood Christmas and birthday experiences were pure magic. I recall the smell of my favorite lasagna my mom made me for my birthday dinner multiple years in a row when I was in elementary school. Or the feeling of walking into my sweet sixteen surprise party in my parent's garage full of my high school friends and a DJ. I remember waking up on my third birthday and seeing our family swing set being built in our backyard. I cried over that swing set as it was taken down twenty-five years later after spending most of my childhood playing on it. I remember feeling sad on my twenty-third birthday for not being with my family while living far away, but my mom had never missed a birthday cake for me, so she had a bakery ship one to me even though I was hundreds of miles away from her.

In all the joy of our childhood Christmas and birthday celebrations, I only remember a few presents. We received wonderful gifts from our parents, grandparents, and extended family over the years, but the memories and experiences have stretched beyond the test of time, lasting longer than any gift could. Now as parents, Jon and I are trying to do the same for our kids.

Presents are the best. The feeling of having an unopened gift in front of you and wondering what could be inside is one of life's most special pleasures. Watching our kids open presents on their birthday or Christmas goes into one of the top tiers of parenthood experiences that never get old. Holidays and birthdays were some of the parts of parenting I was most excited about when we started having kids. I couldn't wait to replicate special experiences from my childhood for our kids. When I dreamed of being a parent, Christmas morning with kids was at the top of that list, knowing that one day I would get to create magic for someone else's childhood just like my parents did for me. I'll never forget our first Christmas with Emily. She was two months old and received more presents than all the grownups combined. It was hilarious yet shocking. How could someone so small need so many presents? (Hint: she didn't *need* any of them.) As we had more kids, the same thing kept happening, but multiplied by more kids and more presents. We were swimming in presents each December. Christmas and birthdays quickly lost a lot of the magic for me, and I became increasingly overwhelmed with trying to figure out how to store all our new gifts. My mom would joke that I was cleaning up Christmas or a birthday before it was over. Are you nodding your head along with me right now? I'm willing to bet you have felt that way at one time or another as a parent.

Dr. Gary Chapman, author of *The 5 Love Languages*, discovered that most people fall into one of five categories when it comes to what makes them feel loved, and everyone has an emotional love tank to express how loved they feel.[15] The love languages are words of affirmation, quality time, acts of service, physical touch, and receiving gifts. Some people may identify with multiple options but typically have just one primary love language. Chapman describes that those who feel loved by receiving gifts view gifts as "visual symbols of love." He explains that "visual symbols of love are more important to some people than others,"[16] and I'm sure you can tell that my love language isn't in the gift category. Gifts are special and important and have proven to transcend cultural boundaries. Whether it's a child opening a box of new MAGNA-TILES® at their birthday party or one child giving another child a stick, gifts are given in every culture. Presents are a universal way of showing love that crosses all borders.

---

15 Gary Chapman, *The 5 Love Languages: The Secret to Love That Lasts* (Chicago: North-field Publishing, 1992).

16 Chapman, *The 5 Love Languages*, 77.

In our culture, holidays and birthdays mean two things: sugar and gifts. We've learned over many generations that to celebrate we must involve one of those two items, neither of which is necessary. While gifts are a wonderful, magical part of many events, they can take away from the true meaning of what is being celebrated. Birthdays are the annual recognition of turning another year older along with remembering past years of life. Birthdays aren't just for the kids, though; they are also milestones for parents. Have you ever wished a mom "Happy birthday" on one of her kid's birthdays? I guarantee you that she's remembering all the effort it took to bring her child into their family, whether biologically or through adoption, and reveling in all the milestones since. On my kids' birthdays, I am extra reflective on all we've been through as a family. I go through newborn pictures and each birthday since then, reminiscing on our growth. Christmas is a religious holiday that commemorates the birth of Jesus, and for our family, it's a time to reflect, practice traditions, and spend time together. Gifts can and should be a part of these momentous occasions, but they don't need to be the primary focus. Let me say that again: *gifts are amazing, but they do not need to be the focus of any event.* (The gift-giving lovers around the world are gasping and giving me the angry eye right now; I can feel it.)

The Four Pillars

There's a time and place for gifts, so the question isn't *whether* we should give gifts to our children; it's the volume of them. How much is enough? As parents, it's our job to show our children where the boundaries are and help them operate within those lines. This applies to saying "no" when your toddler wants to jump off a nine-foot wall as well as determining an appropriate amount of presents under the Christmas tree. In our family, we use the four pillars of gift giving for all gifts from Mom and Dad. The four pillars are:

- ▶ Something they want
- ▶ Something they need
- ▶ Something to wear
- ▶ Something to read

That's it! On any given holiday or birthday, our kids get four presents from Jon and me. When we first implemented this idea, it felt *so* wrong. I felt very guilty as a mom for not giving our kids more gifts, but I quickly learned that opening gifts was sometimes more important to my kids than what was inside the box. Our kids were old enough when we started this to ask if there were more presents to open, but each time we told them that was all, it never went any further. If they start to react negatively and ask for more gifts, there's a lesson we haven't covered yet, and it's a good time to discuss it.

The four pillars concept drastically reduces our spending for holidays and birthdays, along with my stress level for preparing, wrapping, and storage. I take it a step further and wrap all our presents in plain butcher paper, then let each child decorate them before they go under the tree or in front of the birthday child. It makes the moment more special, and they love being involved in the process. Let's break down each of the four pillars.

Something they want. Our kids make a Christmas and birthday list each year, just like every other child, but instead of getting everything on their list, we pick one item that will be most meaningful to them. This also gives us the ability to share ideas with others that will have a big impact while not overdoing the level of gifts.

Something they need. Probably not the most fun of the categories, but this is always my favorite of the gift pillars to give. My kids have received new water bottles, rain boots, bedding, backpacks, and furniture from this category. It also can be a catch-all place to include some nontraditional gift ideas.

Something to wear. This is an easy category to choose from. Kids are always growing, so what would a birthday be without a new outfit? It's practical because you can fill the gaps in their wardrobe, but it's also fun. This is a particular favorite for my kids who wear a lot of hand-me-downs as it guarantees they have new outfits all for themselves.

Something to read. Our kids get a new book from us each on Christmas and their birthday. A lot of times we write a note to them in the front so they can remember the occasion, and my hope is that they associate the evergreen beauty of a book given as a gift. Books are a wonderful way to make someone feel loved, and there's never a short supply of them in our home.

Following this chapter, you'll find a gift idea list for each of the age groups we have covered in this book. Many of those gifts fall into these four pillars. There are plenty of things not included, and it's not a suggestion to purchase everything under each age group. It's just a list of some helpful ideas to pass along or use for yourself when it comes to finding a good gift for a special kid.

The four gift-giving pillars idea goes against *everything* we see, hear, read, and are told about holiday shopping. There's not a single Pinterest list or Amazon catalog that encourages you to give fewer gifts. It is absolutely uncomfortable territory, but it can also have really fruitful results. Each gift has more meaning, and our kids can remember what they were given when someone asks. It can be so deflating as a parent to work hard to make something special only to have it overshadowed by volume. When it comes to buying presents for your kids, try to embrace the idea that less is more and focus on quality or impact over quantity.

Tips for Communicating Boundaries

Grandparents. Extended family. Boundaries around gifts. Is anyone sweating yet? This topic is *tricky*. Some of you may have only picked up this book for this section, and honestly, a whole book could be written on this topic. The problem is that each family is different, so there's truly no one-size-fits-all gift-giving answer. The positive side of this is that no one knows your family better than you do, so who better to communicate with them than you? Remember, gift giving is a way for many people to show they care and love, so sometimes the only correct response is to be grateful (and maybe allow some toys to live in the back of a closet for a little while before they disappear).

At the height of my holiday overwhelm, before we established our gift-giving practices at home, I realized it wasn't just us contributing to my panic. Our kids are so loved and lucky to have extended family who want to give them presents, but those added to the gift count in big numbers. Having extended family who want to give your kids gifts is not a bad thing at all. However, it does fill closets quickly. The first step for us was to minimize what we gave our kids and to tread softly with extended family. We gave our kids fewer gifts before ever asking anyone else to do it. This helped us to know what we wanted out of a gift-giving experience and be able to more easily communicate these ideas to others. Once we had our own practices figured out, we had conversations with extended family members. These were received differently by everyone, but they all were receptive to what we were asking. My four sisters came up with the brilliant idea to do one gift from them collectively for each kid, and that has worked beautifully. Sometimes their gifts are toys or clothes, while other times it's a fun experience or special date. My mother-in-law follows our footsteps and usually gives our kids something from each of the categories, and she always runs ideas by us first. My mom works super hard to find gifts that are impactful but still within our admittedly difficult boundaries.

Gifts are a way for many people to extend their love for others across distances or even just from across the living room. It is a beautiful act to watch someone love your child and want to shower them with gifts. It can also be remarkably stressful as you try to figure out how to store everything. To combat gift overload, there are a few things we do in preparation for each holiday season, most of which have little to do with talking to others. In order for me to comfortably communicate my feelings around gift giving, I want to be sure I've done all I can on my side before ever broaching the topic with someone else.

Tips for Preventing Gift Overload

Pre-event clean out. Around late October or early November and before each birthday, we take inventory. The kids are always involved and willing to help because we phrase this as an opportunity to make more space for new gifts that will be coming soon. I go through everyone's closets to know which new items they might need, we sell or donate unused toys, and we go through our book collection. We make room so come Christmas Day or birthday there's a place for everything.

Make a list. Jon and I keep a running list of gift ideas for each of our children, our entire family, and ourselves. We can easily share gift suggestions with family members for Christmas or a birthday, which can minimize the unnecessary gift clutter. Make sure you don't send your whole list to someone, because you might end up getting everything on the list like we did one year. Send one or two ideas out to anyone who asks, and then mark it off the list to prevent repeats.

Shop early. Along with following our guidelines for shopping within the four pillars, I get all birthday or Christmas shopping done at least a month in advance. Not only does this minimize stress in trying to get prepared, but it also gives me time to offer others ideas I haven't used yet. It also allows me to get gifts I want to give the most before anyone else has purchased them.

Ask for experiences over gifts. We love a good experience as a gift. Memories will last a lifetime, but toys may not, so finding special ways to spend time with those you love is a great gift. A trip to the zoo with grandparents, an adventure with just one parent, or even a museum membership can all be wonderful gifts that don't add to physical clutter in your home. Our kids have had experiences getting their nails painted, going to putt-putt golf, enjoying a special brunch just for them, having sleepovers with family members, and attending musical performances, creating lasting memories for them. Each year our kids get the choice between a birthday party or a special birthday experience. We've had so much fun seeing what they choose, and we always honor their wishes. This isn't just for kids either! Recently my parents took Jon and me to a cooking class for the four of us as a birthday present for me.

Pick some consumable gifts. Sometimes a new coloring book or sticker book can be more exciting than a new toy. Opt for consumable gift options that can be used and then discarded. Coloring books, gift cards, art kits, or stickers are really fun ideas that take up very little space in your home.

Have a plan for your home. Be proactive in knowing where new items will be stored to ease the transition into your home. You will likely not be aware of everything your family will receive, but you can preemptively have a plan for where things will live to make it easier to put them away, including the location of your donation pile.

Be very clear. There's no way around it: if you aren't comfortable with something, you need to communicate those feelings. There's always a kind way to be honest, but if you never say something, how will others know? If you have a great aunt who sends too many gifts, you can graciously say how much you appreciate the love she shows your children but ask if she could please reduce the volume for next time.

Have a set of key phrases to use when expressing your concerns. Always think through what you want to say in advance. It helps to write down key phrases or thoughts to have on hand for difficult conversations. Discuss your talking points in advance with your spouse or another trusted family member to ensure you're being kind but honest.

See the forest for the trees. Sometimes the best thing you can do is realize that you can't change other people. No matter how prepared you are or how well you communicate your feelings, there will still be someone who doesn't want to adhere to your wishes. If that's the case, your best option may be to let it go and move on. I'm willing to bet that more often than not, you'll be able to successfully share your feelings with some members of your family, but there will always be someone who thinks they know better. In those circumstances, remind yourself that they want to give your family gifts because they love you. Just accept the gifts and move on.

LET'S CHOOSE LESS GIFT-GIVING BOUNDARY TOOLS:

- ▶ Have a list handy to offer to others for gift ideas that would work well for your home.
- ▶ Have your home fully prepared in advance for an influx of gifts.
- ▶ Graciously receive all gifts and have a plan for where items will go.
- ▶ Prepare talking points in advance.
- ▶ When all else fails, accept the gifts, and move on.

Unwanted Gifts

Now, for the million-dollar question: What do you do with gifts you don't want? Unwanted gifts are an inevitable part of any holiday or birthday. One of the biggest ways to combat receiving things you don't want is to simply ask for no gifts. It's becoming very popular for parents to request no gifts at birthday parties, which is a brilliantly simple way to reduce gift stress. Even still, there will be gifts given that you may not want, and the most important thing to do is to accept them graciously and then decide what to do with them in private. I save many gifts for rainy or sick days to have new toys or crafts on hand when our kids need some new entertainment. Just because you receive a gift on a certain occasion doesn't mean it has to be opened and used that day as well. A donation pile or a "to be sold" pile are helpful ways of organizing items you may not have a use for in your home. However you choose to use, dispose of, or hide unwanted gifts, I urge you to think of the person who gave the present. If you know this person will want to see your child play or use this item, it may be worthwhile to store it in a closet to use when they are visiting. If it's something that will be given and forgotten about, then don't feel bad for allowing that item to leave your home. Once a gift has been given, it's yours to do with as you decide, so don't allow obligation or pressure to persuade you to act differently.

Gifts come in all forms, shapes, and sizes. The gifts of my childhood that have stayed with me the longest are the memories. Now as a mom, the precious moments and memories far outweigh anything I could open in a box—a wildflower picked just for me; a hug for Mother's Day; a handmade card because I'm "a special mommy;" anything with a handprint, footprint, thumbprint, or any other kind of print. Those gifts are the ones I never want to forget, and I want my kids to feel the same way. A hug for being another year older. A special dinner with just Daddy. A new journal to write down all your dreams. A bike that encourages hours of driveway fun and family bike rides. A trip to Dollar Tree to pick out a treat. An ice cream date with Grandpa. A surprise birthday party. The greatest gift we could ever give someone, especially a child, is time. Ask anyone who has lost someone they love, and I'm willing to bet they would give up all the presents they could ever receive for the rest of their lives for more time with that person. I would gladly never open another box in exchange for a little more time with my grandparents. If we let ourselves get swept into the commercialized whirlwind of gift giving, we may miss out on some of the most cherished gifts of all. Gifts are so special, but as my dad always says, "Too much of anything can be a bad thing." Always try to place the correct emphasis on what celebrations are for and remember that time is the only thing we can't buy more of.

 ## LET'S CHOOSE LESS GIFT-GIVING TIPS:

- ▶ Utilize the four pillars of gift giving.
- ▶ Prepare in advance to allow for less stress and easy budgeting.
- ▶ Involve your kids!
- ▶ Offer ideas to others.
- ▶ Remember what the focus of the event is.
- ▶ Be clear with your boundaries to others but also do what you can on your side to make receiving gifts easier.

Journal Prompts/Discussion Questions:

▶ Do you know what your love language is?

▶ How important are gifts to you?

▶ Do you remember a special gift from your childhood?

▶ What is a special experience you'd like to replicate from your childhood?

FINAL THOUGHTS

—————

This whole project started as a whisper in the back of my mind, and I ignored it for as long as I could. One summer night, my best friend and I were out for a rare kid-free dinner when she pulled out a notebook and said, "Talk, and I'll write out the outline for your book." In a matter of a few minutes, this secret project I had been hiding took a rudimentary shape in front of me on paper. I was terrified and exhilarated at the same time, and then I did nothing about it for months. I was frozen. I attempted to write and rewrite an introduction several dozen times but could never move forward.

Finally, I met with my book coach, Kathy, who helped me see that I would never finish if I didn't get started. Over the next few months, I wrote in stolen moments between parenting my kids. I would steal a half hour hiding in my closet or an afternoon at the library, thanks to Jon. I somehow fit this project in around work commitments, changing diapers, making lunches, and our first full year of homeschooling. It was truly an experiment I created to fit around motherhood.

As the book came into existence, I was still terrified to tell anyone. It took ages to share with anyone around me, and I still felt so hesitant to bring it up. Imposter syndrome is a real roadblock. I'm a mom first and foremost, and I felt like I had no business writing a book. I was afraid no one would want to hear this story. I finally realized I was letting my fears keep me from seeing what could come from trying (which ironically was how we felt when we began our simplifying journey).

Let's Choose Less was born from our family's experience of trying something new and having no idea what we were doing. We went down the path of more resistance by choosing to live differently than most people we knew. It was (and still is) a constant, active effort to stay on track—almost like walking up the down escalator. If we stopped to think about it for too long, we would get swept back into the rush and end up going in the opposite direction of our goals. Yet the more we worked on it, the easier it became. The voices of disagreement around us and in our heads became quieter, and our world seemed to get a little less complicated. Decisions became easier to make. The battles for what our kids chose to wear became less epic, our family was more easily able to let go of unnecessary items that entered our home, we had less physical clutter to keep track of, our calendar became less chaotic, and most importantly, we started getting actual time to rest. Every good practice takes work, and none of these things are permanent. We continue to actively strive for the lifestyle we've designed because if we don't, we will easily end up back where we were. Laundry still piles up, my living room is currently strewn with play trains, and our yard makes it blatantly obvious we have kids with all the toys haphazardly left out in the sun. Yet somehow it seems a little easier to handle, all because we were brave enough to take that first step in being *less*.

You've arrived at the threshold where practice turns into action. You have all the tools, and now it is up to *you* to put them to work. The more you practice, the easier it will become, but you must take that first step. All the best-laid plans are still plans until they are executed. Learn from my mistakes and act now rather than wait. (Remember, there will never be a "good" time to start. You have to just dive in!)

Once you begin, the proverbial snowball will start rolling. First, it will be a clean drawer in your kitchen, and then it will spread. Soon you'll know exactly where to put things in your home, you'll be able to pack for trips like a champion, you'll be more prepared to decline social obligations, and you'll have a clear understanding of your gift-giving policy for birthdays and holidays. Your friends will ask how you found time to rest on a weekday afternoon or how you seem to be a little less stressed than before. Share what you've learned. Show them! Ask them the discussion questions. Some of the best advice I've ever heard is that if you want to learn about something, find someone to teach it to. Grab your best friend and clean out a closet together. Nothing says friendship like being knee-deep in baby clothes that need to be sorted. Not everyone lives this way. This lifestyle is a gift, and its value lies in being shared.

In a world that asks us to be more, do more, buy more, and constantly up the ante, I'm here to say that you can be a great parent but not adhere to the parameters that society has imposed on you. *Let's Choose Less* teaches us that we can love our kids but not smother them in stuff. We can take an active stance on doing fewer activities in exchange for more family time, we can communicate healthy gift-giving boundaries, and we can actively choose to have less stuff in our homes. Life is complicated enough, so let's strip away the excess and live purposely in the essentials. Join me, friend, and together we can choose to lose and pursue less together.

ACKNOWLEDGMENTS

———

None of this would have been possible without the love and support of my closest inner circle and the grace of God.

I am humbled and grateful to be on this journey with my soul mate, Jonathan. His impeccable ability to ask questions and brainstorm these ideas together is how this entire project came about. I love you with all my heart, Jon. You're my favorite person ever. Our precious children and their beautiful messes have given us the perfect slate on which to learn together. Emily, Sophie, Maggie, and Jay, may you always know how special you are, and I thank God every day for sending you to us. Each of you is the perfect addition to our family, and without you, we would not be us.

To Kathy, Amanda, Linda, Claudia, and George for your guidance, editing, and willingness to answer all my questions will never be forgotten. This project was completed thanks to you all.

To my mom, dad, sisters, and in-laws, thank you for listening to me talk about this when I was too afraid to tell anyone else. You had more of an impact than you realize in helping me find my voice.

To my friends, thank you for reading random chapters, remembering funny stories I'd forgotten, double-checking all my lists, and showing me unconditional love. I think we need a girls' weekend to celebrate.

To you, my dear reader and now friend, thank you for delving into this process with me and for hearing our story. I hope it has made you smile and encouraged you to think a little deeper about what's truly important to you and your family.

APPENDIX

Let's Choose Less Baby Registry

Need to Have	Nice to Have
Crib	Bottle sample kit
Pack-n-play	Pacifier sample kit
Car seat	Stroller
High chair	Humidifier
Diapers and wipes	Baby monitor
Diaper cream	Diaper bag
Clothes (10 to 12 outfits per size/season)	Board books
Baby blankets	Breastfeeding pillow
Baby wrap or carrier	
Baby first aid (Band-Aids, infant Tylenol, Benadryl, saline drops/spray)	
Baby grooming supplies (shampoo, lotion, nail trimmer, booger suction)	
Postpartum supplies (such as Frida Mom postpartum recovery kit)	
Nursing/pumping bras	

Let's Choose Less Gift Ideas

Something they want
Something they need
Something to wear
Something to read

Gifts for All Ages	Baby Gift List
Books	Low mirror
Anything water play-related	Play mat
Puzzles	Play food and kitchen supplies
Art supplies	Teething toys
Building supplies	Push toys
Baby dolls	Stacking toys
Clothes/shoes/coats	Indestructible books
Sporting gear (balls, goals, nets)	Black-and-white books
Experiences	Textured toys and books
Memberships	
Subscriptions	

Age One Gift List	Age Two Gift List
Musical instruments	Rain boots/raincoat/umbrella
Learning tower	Sidewalk chalk
Peg puzzles	Playdough
Threading games	Play trains
Pikler® climbing gym and slide	Balance bike
Construction vehicles	Coloring books and art supplies
Kid-sized table and chair set	Kitchen tools for kids
Cleaning materials	Personalized placemat
Beeswax crayons	Dot markers
Finger paint	Sandbox
Wagon	Toniebox® (audio player)
Tricycle	T-ball set
Water table	Wheelbarrow
Water bottle	Digger for dirt or sand play
Watering can	Tool kit
	Indoor slide

Age Three Gift List	Age Four Gift List
Wood building blocks	DUPLO® building bricks
Scooter	Lincoln Logs
Personalized name puzzle	MAGNA-TILES®
Easel and art supplies	Bicycle
Zippered bedding	Beanbag chair
Nugget® Play Couch	Kinetic sand
Kid-sized golf set	Marble kit
Dress-up clothes/accessories	Watch
Water wall	Ninja course
Obstacle course supplies	Traffic cones for imaginative play
Personalized cup	Seeds and flower planting supplies
Gardening supplies	Sprinkler
Play tent	Sports equipment (balls, bats, nets, goals)
	Yoto Player® (audio player)

Age Five Gift List
LEGO® bricks
Backpack/purse
Embroidered apron
Alarm clock
Watercolor painting kit
Playmobil® kits
Nature journals
Board games
Fairy garden supplies
Storybutton® (audio player)

LET'S CHOOSE LESS
ADDITIONAL READING

———

Secondhand: Travels in the New Global Garage Sale by Adam Minter

The Montessori Toddler: A Parent's Guide to Raising a Curious and Responsible Human Being by Simone Davies

The Nesting Place: It Doesn't Have to Be Perfect to Be Beautiful by Myquillyn Smith

Minimalist Moms: Living and Parenting with Simplicity by Diane Boden

The Family Firm: A Data-Driven Guide to Better Decision Making in the Early School Years by Emily Oster

Cribsheet: A Data-Driven Guide to Better, More Relaxed Parenting, from Birth to Preschool by Emily Oster

Messy Minimalism: Realistic Strategies for the Rest of Us by Rachelle Crawford

A Simpler Motherhood: Curating Contentment, Savoring Slow, and Making Room for What Matters Most by Emily Eusanio

Essentialism: The Disciplined Pursuit of Less by Greg McKeown

Birth Story by Heidi Snyderburn

The Read-Aloud Family: Making Meaningful and Lasting Connections with Your Kids by Sarah Mackenzie

Hunt, Gather, Parent: What Ancient Cultures Can Teach Us About the Lost Art of Raising Happy, Helpful Little Humans by Michaeleen Doucleff

Balanced and Barefoot: How Unrestricted Outdoor Play Makes for Strong, Confident, and Capable Children by Angela J. Hanscom

Wise Moms: A Guide for Building Your Home on Christ by Linda Ruth Reeb

ABOUT THE AUTHOR

 **Jenna Michael** is a wife, mother, author, and coach specializing in simplified and intentional living for families. Her writing covers topics such as family-friendly activities and events, wellness, travel, gifts, and essential parenting tips. Her coaching helps moms turn these valuable insights into practical action, reduce clutter and chaos, and ultimately pursue a life *of* purpose *on* purpose. In her free time, you can find her at the gym, curled up with a book, or enjoying the outdoors.

For more information about Jenna and her work, visit **yourpurposefulparenting.com.**

www.ingramcontent.com/pod-product-compliance
Lightning Source LLC
Chambersburg PA
CBHW061727120626
46550CB00005B/1731